COUNTRY PUNKIN

As I sit here on a lonely, sandy beach in Southwest Michigan, gazing out over the great vastness of Lake Michigan, I am feeling somewhat nostalgic. I tell myself, surely there is more to life than just beating your brains out to pay the bills, having a few kids, gathering a few things along life's road and then dying. Did you ever wonder how, of all the places on planet earth, you ended up where you are? Did you ever pause to ruminate how fortunate some people are in comparison to others? Have you ever reminisced about your lifetime and asked yourself, "What is it really all about?" I often marvel why we get into these moods; you know what I mean, wanting to be somewhere else but not really wanting to leave. Wanting to do something else, or be like someone else. What makes us think that the grass is always greener on the other side of the fence?

As I sit here on the sand with my shoes off and my feet buried in the sand, I feel a serenity or satisfaction that comes from a peace of mind. As I pick up a hand full of sand and let it run through my fingers, the sea gulls are flying about, looking for scraps that may have been left behind by the sunbathers from the day before.

I just left a nearby factory where I work the midnight shift. A breeze is coming off the lake with just a little nip in it, being the beginning of fall. I often come here to unwind and get alone with God. As I look out over the deep blue lake I can see a few sailboats already heading for the open water as this new day begins.

Have you ever pondered over your life and thought of all the things you would have changed? As I muse over my last forty four years, I can honestly say it hasn't been boring.

As I meditate on life, I realize that it is short compared with eternity. The Bible states that life is like a vapor, that appeareth for a little time, and then vanisheth away. Sometimes when I get into these moods I regret the time I lost doing things which didn't contribute to life in general. I've been told that the older one gets, the more life seems short and precious. Middle age is a perplexing time of life when we hear two voices calling us; one saying "why not?" and the other saying, "why bother?"

On my forty-forth birthday I asked my wife, "Do you realize how many people die before they reach my age?" Athletes, movie stars, rich people and poor ones too, no one seems exempt. We have no promise of tomorrow. We live in a day and age where all it would take is for one wild man to push a button and begin a nuclear war. As I sit here on this peaceful, tranquil beach there is no less than 250,000 American troops congregating in Saudi Arabia. Who knows what the future holds for those troops or for the world, as far as that is concerned.

As I reflect back in time, I have been told that I was born on the other side of this very lake in Chicago, Illinois; just a few years after the Japanese bombed Pearl Harbor. My father, like most everyone else in those days, went into the military to do his part for the cause of freedom and the American way.

My days in the big city were short for, when I was three years old, my folks packed up all they owned and headed for the country. The rat race

2

wasn't for my folks. It has been said that the only ones who can win in a rat race are the rats. We headed southeast into Indiana and ended up in a little town called North Judson. My folks had dreams and expectations of making a go of it outside the big city. As in most small towns in America, if you want an acceptable paying job, you have to commute to the noisy city. I am grateful to Dad for taking us out of the city while I was still young, before I became one of the rats in the rat race in the hustle and bustle of Chicago living.

We had a mini ten-acre farm outside of town. It had a few animals; a couple dogs, a few rabbits, and a pig or two. We had a small garden every year full of potatoes, tomatoes, beans and peas; you know, the typical farmer's garden to help lighten the load around dinner- time.

I have two brothers; one older, Bill, who is a helicopter mechanic in the state of Georgia, and a younger brother, Howard. I can't call him a little brother anymore, his being 6'4" and 230 lbs. I have one sister, Patricia, whom we all call "Candy."

As I look back on those days on that small farm, I see now that we "had it made". We had plenty of kids to play with in our neighborhood. One particular family was the Bell's. They were the kind of family that every neighborhood has, perhaps you know the type, where everybody hangs out. They were the first ones to have a television set. We had a baseball diamond behind their house and a basketball hoop. The Bell's always had all of the latest in balls and gloves. We used to call this piece of planet earth "Bell Stadium."

One day one of the Bell boys, I'm not sure if it was Danny or Larry, and myself decided that we were going to plant a watermelon patch. We both liked watermelon, and besides, we may have felt a little guilty for stealing most of Mr. Lemke's watermelons the night before. We took a couple shovels and went up on top of a small hill where we started spading up the ground for our watermelon plantation. After about ten minutes I developed a blister on my right hand. I showed off my blister to my partner and he said, "There must be a better way to do this than all this hard work." We sat down and thought it over for a few minutes, and then it dawned on us what the answer was. Why not burn off the weeds, then we could spade it up after that.

I ran home and went into the kitchen where I helped myself to a fistful of kitchen matches. I ran back to the top of our little hill where my partner was waiting patiently. After we decided just how big we wanted our patch to be, we dragged our shovels in the ground and drew the perimeter. We fired it up. At first it wouldn't burn very well, so we put dead weeds over the smoldering fire. All of a sudden it took off, and when it came to the outer boundaries of our garden, it just kept on going. It seemed as though the wind was blowing a lot stronger than when we first began.

Within half an hour we had three fire trucks from two neighboring towns fighting the blaze. I had learned my first Biblical principle. "Be sure your sins will find you out."

People for miles around came to help save the community. I will never forget looking through the blaze and smoke, and seeing my Dad. He had a wet gunny -sack in one hand and was shaking his fist at me with the other. He was screaming at me, " I'm going to kill you, I'm going to kill you!"

I don't know what the big deal was; all we did was burn down the neighbor's apple orchard, plus we almost took his house with it. There was a wooded area nearby and about five acres were destroyed, plus about three acres of grassland.

After the fire looked as though it might be under control, I thought to myself, "If I'm ever going to run away from home, this would be a good time to do it." So off I went. I headed down the hill and across the already burnt grasslands. It was hours later that I saw the house of a friend of mine who rode on the same school bus with me. The name of my friend is Ronnie Minix. Ronnie had four or five brothers and two or three sisters, so one more wouldn't make that much difference. I stayed there for the next three days. I found out later that my folks learned where I was a few hours after I took off, but they decided it might be a good idea to give themselves time to cool down. After much persuasion from Ronnie's parents, I went home. As I was walking through the woods on my way home, I was thinking about what I was going to say to Mom and Dad. I thought of all kinds of excuses, but nothing sounded as though it would make any difference.

The first thing I did was to go into the house to see my Mother. If anyone would understand it would be Mom. The first thing she told me was to go out into the garage and see Dad. As I was walking toward the garage, the thought crossed my mind to head for the woods again. The distance from the house to the garage was about a hundred feet, but that day it seemed like it was attached to the house.

About the time I had decided to run for my life, Dad came around the corner of the building. He had a sledge hammer in his hand. He had a project in the garage he had been pounding on, and perspiration was running off his forehead. He looked at me, his eyes seemed like they were going to pop out of his head, and he made a fist with his free hand and said, The only reason I'm not going to beat you is because I'm afraid I would kill you."

I was grounded for months, but that was better than facing Dad's belt. The one thing Dad taught me during the time I was grounded was to be obedient to authority.

Obedience, I have learned over the years, is one of the most important things we can teach our children. If a child is obedient to his parents, he will be obedient to the authority of his teacher , thus making him a better student. If a child is obedient to the authority of his parents, he will be more apt to be obedient later on in life to the authority of the police officer, thus making him a good citizen. If a father and mother teach their child to submit to their authority young enough, he will grow to submit to the supreme authority, which is the Word of God, thus enabling him to become a

5

more useful and productive Christian.

As I look back on that little ten-acre farm, I remember life being happy and carefree. I suppose that is what life is to a ten year old boy who has all his dreams and expectations ahead of him. It is always easier to look back on life when all we usually remember are the good times. Do you reckon that is why we fondly refer to them as "the good old days?"

HAPPY

I don't believe I will ever forget about the time when my Dad was going to go into the chicken business. He had scraped up enough extra money to invest in one hundred and fifty baby chicks. When we first bought them they were so cute and cuddly. Dad was so proud of them, he had the neighbor over and took him down into our Michigan-type basement where the chicks were, to show them off. Dad had bought two or three heat lamps and had them hanging over the chicks in one corner of the basement. After a couple of weeks they had grown quite a bit.

One day we all loaded up in our big shiny black 1945 Buick, and went into town to buy some supplies for our new enterprise. Dad explained to me how we would sell the chickens at the market, along with the eggs, and how some of the eggs would hatch and give us more chickens. "It's simple," he said. After arriving home from town, he went down into the basement. On his way down the stairs, Happy, the family dog was on his way up the stairs. Dad went to his favorite corner of the basement, and when he arrived he saw a terrible sight; one hundred and fifty dead chickens! Happy had gotten to those baby chicks and had mauled them to death. Happy was one of those Heinz 57 variety mutts; you know the kind, so homely that you couldn't help but love him.

All of a sudden Dad started yelling and screaming, cursing every breath. We all ran downstairs to see what on earth the problem was. Dad was in a rage. He ran up the stairs and went into his and Mom's bedroom to get the only gun we owned, an old 22 rifle; the type that had to be loaded after every shot. We all knew what he had in mind, and it didn't look good for poor old Happy. As Dad started chasing Happy around the house, my big brother Billy and I started chasing him. We were crying our eyes out, begging him not to shoot Happy. Dad was chasing Happy, we were chasing Dad, and Mom was chasing us. He would take a shot at that mutt, then he would have to stop and reload, and we would catch up with him, and with Billy on one leg and me on the other, we would beg him not to shoot Happy. Finally after several rounds around the house, my mother caught up with him. Somehow she persuaded him not to kill Happy; at least not in front of us kids.

Dad went stomping off into the house, mad as a hornet. About an hour and thirty minutes, and six beers later, he went down in the basement and gathered up all the little dead chickens. He then went out into the garage, found a fifty-five gallon drum, and put those chickens in it. He then put the drum out in the middle of a field about three or four hundred yards from the house. After much coaxing, he talked Happy into going to him. That poor mutt must have had a guilty conscience, because he went almost crawling to Dad with his tail between his legs. Then Dad grabbed him and took him out into the middle of the field and put him in that 55-gallon drum with all those dead chickens. Dad put a couple pieces of chicken wire over the top of the drum, then a house block on top of that to hold it in place.

About three days later, as the sun went down and a breeze kicked up, you could smell the results of Happy's rampage as the wind blew from that direction.

Finally, on the fifth day, Dad took a long narrow board and went out to the drum. By this time the smell was so bad that I had to hold my breath to keep from gagging. Dad tipped the drum over, and out come poor Happy, covered with feathers and maggots. He hit the ground on a run!

I will say this for Happy, he never bothered chickens anymore. As a matter of fact, if he saw an egg he would run the other way. The whole episode was enough to discourage dear old Dad out of the chicken business.

It was about this time in my young life that I came across my first encounter with church. I was invited to go to the home of one of our neighbors where they were going to have church. Frank, who invited me, lived on a small hill, off from a small gravel road, about a quarter of a mile from our house. Frank's parents were poor folk, like most of us, who had moved up from Kentucky. They lived in a small, two-bedroom shack with an outhouse in the back yard. Boys being boys, we used to peek through the cracks in the boards of the outhouse when Frank's older sister would go in there.

When we arrived at Frank's house there was a tall, slim man standing in the yard smoking a cigarette. I learned later that he was a preacher. We went into the living room where there were chairs all around the walls with nothing in the middle. We sat down, and a few minutes later the preacher came in. He stood in the middle of the room and said a few words, and then he said a prayer. After the prayer I noticed the preacher had stuck his left hand down in the front of the waist-band of his pants. He started speaking very softly, so that I could barely hear him, and then he became louder and louder. Within a few minutes he had raised his right hand into the air and was waving it wildly. He would say two or three sentences, until he ran out of breath, then he would stop and suck in all the air he could, then spit out two or three more sentences. This he did several times. After awhile he had gotten a rhythm. His face was beet- red. By this time all the people in the room were yelling, "Amen," "Hallelujah," and "Praise the Lord!"

I was terrified as this wild man, with one hand in his pants and the other hand waving in the air, was running around that little room. I learned later that this type of preacher is referred to as a "hack preacher" by folks from the deep-south.

I remember bowing my head, as I was too scared to look up or around, and holding my hands together on my lap, hoping I wouldn't do anything that would draw attention to myself. I thought "If this is church, I don't want any part of it!" After what seemed like forever, it was finally over. As soon as I saw my chance, I headed for the door, and I ran home as fast as my little legs would carry me.

It has been said that first impressions are lasting impressions, and I am afraid it is true. I didn't have anything to do with church, or God, for the next twenty years.

LEARNING THE HARD WAY

Living in the country had it's advantages and disadvantages. My brothers and I learned all about that four- letter word work. I am concerned that it isn't in the vocabulary of most young people today.

We burned wood to heat our home. Our neighbor had about twenty acres of woodland, and he too heated his home by burning wood. We helped each other cut enough wood to last a week. I didn't mind cutting wood on the weekend, but to a twelve-year old boy, every weekend was a bit much. Every Saturday we would get all bundled up, go out and cut wood for the week.

One Saturday a couple buddies of mine talked me into playing basketball in a fellow's barn a couple of miles down the same gravel road we lived on. At the time, it sounded like a great idea to me. So, instead of heading for the woods, I headed for the barn. I had a great time with the guys, and besides, I had needed a break.

Needless to say, when I returned home Dad was waiting for me. After he called me into the garage, he asked if I helped cut wood. I never would lie to him, and I didn't then as I answered, "No sir." He said, "Where in — —were you?"

"I was playing basketball with the guys," I replied. Somehow he looked a lot bigger than his six feet, two hundred and fifty pounds frame as he told me to hold out my hands. As I reached out my hands, he picked me up with his left hand and removed his belt with his right hand. There is a saying, "A strap in the hand is worth two courses in child psychology." How true that is! Dad strapped me good, and, as I look back on it, I realize I deserved it.

I learned another Biblical principle that day. What one sows is what one reaps. We get out of life what we put into it. If a person expects respect, he or she must show respect. In order receive love, one needs to show love. Those who continually try to jab people, most assuredly, will get jabbed back sooner or later.

I believe a large number of people go through life unhappy and disappointed because they believe others treat them unfairly. True joy and contentment, I've learned, come when people put others first. There would not be as many nervous breakdowns and medicine cabinets wouldn't resemble a doctor's office if individuals would stop worrying about themselves and think of others. The happiest time of the year for most of us is at Christmas time. We are thinking of others as we buy gifts for our friends and loved ones. If we stop and think about what really makes us happy, we could have Christmas 365 days a year. The Bible states, "It is more blessed to give than to receive."

We eventually sold that ten-acre farm that meant so much to me and moved into town. Dad bought what had been a lumber- yard, and we converted the office into our home and the outbuilding into Dad's repair shop. Dad would work all day making railroad box cars, some thirty-five miles away, then come home and work in his shop until late at night.

After we moved into town, we no longer had to ride on the school bus. The school where we attended was approximately one half mile from our house, so we were able to walk to school.

My mother worked in a convalescent home in a small town seven miles away from our home. She eventually got us all working there before we grew up and went out on our own. I worked in the kitchen washing pots and pans. I ate everything I could get my hands on. Most of the kids my age were working in the peppermint and spearmint fields, pulling weeds.

After I had gotten a few paychecks I decided I would purchase myself a car. With the help of my folks I bought my first car; a 1955 Chevy convertible. It was a beautiful blue with a white top. Even though the top didn't always go up right, it was still a convertible. There was a big pair of white fluffy dice hanging over the rearview mirror. I took the hub- caps off and painted the hubs black. That really made those white wall tires stand out!

The very first day after I bought the car, two or three other guys on the block and myself decided to cut classes. We had a principal in our high school that took his job seriously. We were in my back yard putting on about the third coat of wax on my car when in pulled the principal and vice-principal. Boy, we sure were surprised to see them!

As they drove in we all ran into the house to hide, but eventually, because it was my house, I had to answer the door. They told me they had seen the others as they pulled in, and we were to report to their office first thing the next morning. After they left, we finished waxing the car, and then someone suggested, seeing as how we were caught anyway, why not take a spin? We put the top down on the car and headed up town. As we were driving past the high school, some of the guys saw us and stuck their heads out of the window, giving us a thumbs-up sign. I didn't want to disappoint anyone so I stopped, backed up, and dropped that hot rod Chevy into low gear. I left about ten pounds of rubber on the street, accompanied by blue smoke. I made a squealing noise that could be heard for miles. I was the hero of the entire school for the rest of that day. The next day dawned, and we had to face the music. Somehow I didn't feel like Mr. Popularity anymore. Funny how life is sometimes; it seems as though we never think of the results of our actions until it is too late. The real punishment came days later when my folks found out about the whole thing!

THE GLORY DAYS

My home town is typical of all small towns, especially in the state of Indiana, where basketball is king. There is only one traffic light in the whole town, and that is a flashing red light. Just recently they have put stop signs up at most of the corners on the main drag.

This small town, like most, doesn't have much going on for the teenagers. Every weekend the entire town is taken over by the teenagers, driving their freshly waxed cars around on the same streets. The adults are in the same kind of a rut, usually flocking to the local bars while their teenagers are out in the night, making their own fun. Not much to look forward to, is it?

A survey was once taken, calling people on the telephone at 11:00 p.m., asking them if they knew where their teenagers were. Sixty-five percent of the telephone calls were answered by children who didn't know where their parents were that Saturday night.

The high school was the largest building in town, having three stories. We had two lumber yards, a few stores, one theater, a couple of gas stations, four or five bars, and as many churches.

The nearest decent paying job was about twenty miles away, unless you were one of the select few in town who owned your own business. Industry has tried to come into town, but the town-board, which was also the town's business owners, was afraid it would attract undesirables. Now, years later, those same businessmen and businesswomen are crying the blues because their children are scattered all over the United States where they can make a decent living. As I reflect back on my days growing up in a small town like that, I suppose I have become a little bitter with some of the decisions that some of the townsfolk made.

All the predominancy in the community was, and is, centered around sports and talent. I was fortunate in that I was six feet, two inches tall and could walk and chew gum at the same time, making me one of the favorites in town.

I believe the happiest days of my young life were the ones in my junior year in high school. I was popular, I had the prettiest girlfriend in the whole school, and I could play basketball. I could go into town and the merchants would give me free haircuts, clothes, and even a hamburger every now and then. All this was because I had the potential to put their little hick town on the map through basketball.

Each year the townspeople would look for the great white hope, who would score big, go off to college, and then the professionals. But year after year they were disappointed; but maybe, who knows, this could be the one (referring to me}. This was a time when I went to school when I had a ball game, or a test I had to take to stay on the team. Being a future star was important to these folks, and I could do no wrong.

When I did make a mistake in a basketball game, people would say, "Just wait until next year, he is young yet, give him time." When I had a good game they would say, "Just wait until next year, he is going to break the school scoring record." Those were good days, life was carefree, and it seemed as though everybody was my friend.

One day my sweetheart and I came strolling into history class, late as usual, and took our seats. The teacher, who was also the basketball coach, asked in a stern voice, "Margie, do you have Larry's homework done?" She smiled real pretty, batted those big, blue eyes, and answered, "Yes sir."

He replied, "That a girl!" This is typical of most public school systems in America today. Most, if not all, of the emphasis is placed on one's talent, not one's character. No one seemed to think it was important that I showed up late all the time, or that I was just getting by with my grades in order to stay on the team. Most of my time was spent across the street from the high school at the local hang out. School, for the most part, was a joke to me. Yes, my junior year in high school brings back some fond memories.

My senior year, on the other hand, was a disaster! Those same people who bragged on me the year before, became my biggest critics. If I scored twenty-five points in a ball game, it should have been thirty-five points. If I had a bad game, then I was considered just another loser; like most before me.

I hated to go downtown any more. People would tell me about how they would have done it differently had they been in my shoes. In my senior year I had all the pressures on me because there wasn't going to be a next year. I had to produce now, or never! I was always in the principal's office for something, and each time I was threatened with being kicked off the team. I became paranoid and was a nervous wreck. How could all those people turn on me? It was because I wasn't meeting their expectations of being their knight in shining armor that their attitude changed toward me.

As I look back, I can remember dozens of others who were in the same dilemma as myself. I suppose I will never know of all the hurt and rejection felt by those who have been victimized by this way of reasoning.

Yes, there have been two or three who have blossomed into college stars and are forever enshrined as their paragons. But most of us were rejected, even despised, because of our so- called "failures" in their eyes.

These were some traumatic experiences in my young and tender life, and I wasn't mature enough to handle them. Even after twenty-five years I still have some scars, but perhaps they will help in rearing my children, teaching them that having character is more important than having talent!

There was a ray of hope for me as the one who would draw attention to the community by way of sports. In my senior year of high school, while on the track team, I did break the high-jump record. Not only that, but at that time in 1965 I had the highest leap in the entire state at six feet, five and one quarter inches. This brought some recognition to the town, but people there weren't interested in track and field.

As I recall, the very next track meet after I had broken the school record was a home meet. We would run from the high school to the track and field area, approximately one quarter of a mile away. By this time word had gotten out there was a kid called "Leapin Larry" on the team who had gotten some statewide recognition in the high jump.

While we were running onto the track, I was leading the pack; after all, I was the star. The spectators were all standing and applauding as we entered. As we turned the corner onto the cinder track, there was a cable stretched across the road about two feet high. As I approached this cable I jumped over it; well, almost over it. I became entangled in it and fell flat on my face. I was embarrassed to death in front of all those people. High jump hero, what a joke!

Every small town has a place where everybody hangs out; the place where one can go when they can't afford to do anything else. Our hangout was a little hamburger joint across from the high school by the name of Camino's. At lunch time, during school days, there was so much smoke rolling out of the front door from kids smoking, that it looked as if the place was on fire.

It was owned by a chubby little Italian by the name of Tony Camino and his wife, Aggie. They were like second parents to us. We could talk to them and not be afraid of being found out. Camino's is where I first laid eye on the most beautiful girl in the world. She had big blue eyes and long reddish hair. She was a knockout with a body that would catch any man's eye. We started going steady after a few weeks. I knew from the start that she was a special gal.

Her parents, I thought, were a little strange. They didn't allow her to date, even though she was seventeen years old. I would call her on the phone and tell her to meet me at Camino's, and she would tell her parents that she was going uptown to buy a loaf of bread. I often wondered what her parent's thought when she would return hours later without any bread.

Her parents were very religious and didn't want her to date anyone who wasn't a Christian. They would go to church in a building not far from Camino's. It wasn't even a real church building. After a long battle with her parents, she finally asked me to go to church with her. I was so embarrassed! What if the guys from Camino's would see me going to church in that old rickety building?

I used to think to myself, "Why can't these people go to church like normal people, in a church building with pews, piano, and people?" Her parents were determined to make me a Christian, and I was determined to get that gal. I did; they didn't!

I can remember in my earlier teen years of hanging out with the big boys at Camino's. One of my heroes was a fellow named Bill Crowley. He was so cool, he always wore a white tee-shirt, an old black leather jacket, levi's, white socks, and black motorcycle boots. He was like the Fonz on the television show, "Happy Days." He always had some yarn about fast cars and fast women.

I would think to myself, some day I'm going to be just like Bill Crowley. As the years passed I grew up and bought myself a leather jacket (imitation, of course) and hung out with my hero. We told so many yarns I don't know to this day what was true and what was fantasy.

But as time went on I continued on with life; eventually getting a job, a car, a sweetheart, then a wife, children, and responsibilities. I didn't have time to hang out anymore. Life was passing me by, and I wanted to make the most of it. Sad, but true, Bill didn't see life that way. After twenty-five years I can go back to my home town and to Camino's, even though the name has been changed several times, and Bill is still hanging out, and has been married and divorced several times. He still goes to all the ball games, sits in the same section, and is still eyeing little high school girls.

Bill never left that fantasy he was in years earlier; it has been his lifestyle since the early sixties. He never had a real job, never really accepted any kind of responsibility. But if I am honest with myself, I sometimes envy Bill; especially when the pressures come and the responsibilities mount up. Every now and again there arises someone in your childhood, or in your teenage years, that has forced his or her way to the top. Someone who has seemed to have all the breaks in life going for them. If any one person has done anything about putting that little town on the map, besides some great basketball players, it is probably a friend of mine by the name of Jim Kersting. Jim was just one of the guys, not exceptionally intelligent, but not dumb by any stretch of the imagination. I suppose one could say Jim just had good old God given common sense.

Jim had a dream; to stay out of the factories and make a living doing something that he enjoyed doing. Jim was always tinkering around motor-cycles. Back in those days the only real motorcycle in America was the Harley Davidson. Jim had set up a little motorcycle shop on a little side road four miles out of town. We would drive by it every time we went into town from our ten-acre farm. Dad commented as we passed by, "He is going to starve to death out here in the country; besides, no one is going to buy motorcycles now-days."

One summer I had made some extra money weeding peppermint on a farm not far from where I lived. I went over to Jim's to see what kind of a deal I could strike up with him on a motorcycle. About an hour later I rode out of there on a 1920 Harley Indian. It had a 1942 Harley Davidson Engine. It was one of Harley Davidson's first shaft- driven motorcycles. Because the body and the engine were different, Jim had rigged up a driving device using two Allis-Chalmers straw spreader gears.

19

It was a sight. It was red where the paint was and red where the rust was. Jim gave me a couple extra spreader gears to use until I learned how to engage it into drive. The first day I sheared two of the gears trying to get it in drive.

As I remember, my first ride on it was out of his driveway, across the road, and into the ditch where it burst into flames. Jim had forgotten to reinstall the carburetor caps The front tire had a big knot on it, leaving the inner tube bare. If I would go over forty miles per hour it would bounce so bad that it became uncontrollable. If memory serves me correctly, I gave Jim forty-five dollars for it. I was a proud owner of an American made Harley Davidson!

Jim told me years later that he can still see me in his mind's eye as I drove off bouncing down the road, heading home. He said I looked like I was riding a bucking bronco.

The Harley Davidson representative told Jim if he could sell three new Harley's his first two years, he would probably be able to survive in the Harley business. Jim told me that his first year in the business he sold twelve new and several used ones. This got Jim off to a good start. Now Kersting's Cycle Center, even though it's still on that same side road four miles out of town, it is one of the largest cycle shops in Northern Indiana. Jim advertises on radio, and television in Chicago and other large cities.

Jim Kersting is my kind of people. He had a dream and went after it. It has been said, "If you want to fulfill your dream, wake up!"

In Northern Indiana one doesn't have a lot of choices to make as far as what to do when getting out of high school. One choice would be to go to college, but I had goofed off most of my high school days and couldn't pass the entrance exam if I wanted to. The other choice was the steel mills or some other type of factory. I took the easy way out and found a job working in a factory.

When folks found out that I went to work in a factory, some wouldn't even talk to me. I was just like all the rest of the basketball players before me; a loser. The day after I graduated, I moved out of that miserable little one horse town and vowed never to return. As I mentioned earlier, perhaps I am still a little bitter because of those frustrating experiences of my adolescent years.

21

WORLD TRAVELER

Life is full of unexpected events, and for me and thousands of others like me, Vietnam was one of those events. It was the mid-sixties and most of my buddies were getting drafted or joining the service. Vietnam was hot and heavy, and no single person under the age of twenty stood a chance of not going. Just about the time you think you have all the answers in life, somebody changes the questions.

I was just starting out on life. I was making more money than ever before and had just bought myself a 1960 Chevy convertible. I was working at the Ford Motor Stamping Plant in Chicago Heights, Illinois.

Some of my old classmates and myself were living in an apartment in the big city. We would go down to the local pool hall and watch the big city thugs curse and fight over their pool games. This was an exciting night out on the town for this small-town boy. Everything seemed as though it was falling into place. My sweetheart and I had talked about marriage, but neither of us was ready for that big plunge.

As time went by I realized that sooner or later I was going to be drafted. Two days before I received my draft notice into the Army, I joined the

Navy. Military life for this small-town hick was a real shock! I never realized how much of a sheltered life I had led until that time. It was Valentine's Day, 1966, when I said goodbye to my sweetheart and climbed on the bus bound for Chicago and the Great Lakes Naval Training Center.

It was miserably cold that first day, being –27 degrees. The snow was frozen, and it would make a crunching noise when you walked on it. Some of the men in my outfit had flown in from sunny California, and they had their summer clothes on. Sometimes we would have to stand out in the weather for over an hour just to eat. We did not receive our Navy issue gear until after the first or second week there. Our company commander was a little loud mouth fellow from Jersey. He never talked, he yelled!

We once had a surprise inspection in our barracks. When the C.O. inspected a locker he would throw everything out on the deck after looking it over. We were taught to fold all our clothes Navy style. There were three of us that day that failed to fold our skivvies just right. After much yelling and cursing, we were commanded to march to battalion headquarters. Myself, and the two other unfortunates who had flunked the inspection, had the privilege of leading the company to headquarters.

When we finally arrived, the three of us were ordered to stand on the cement apron in front of headquarters. There were three four-foot high torpedoes (unarmed, I hope) standing on a platform. We were ordered to hold those torpedoes over our heads (being fresh out of high school I was still in pretty good shape, being an athlete and all) so, this never bothered me until we were ordered to start doing jumping jacks with the torpedoes being held over our heads. So there we were, the three of us, standing on a concrete apron overlooking the rest of the company who were looking on in complete amazement.

The fellow to the right of me was overweight, and it was obvious that he was out of shape. After about thirty seconds of holding that torpedo over his head, or about the second jumping jack, he dropped the torpedo on his head and knocked himself out. The torpedo went rolling down the steps into the onlookers, soon followed by that dude.

Looking back on life is a lot easier than living it. That occurrence seems funny now; but back in those days it was terrifying. It is these types of experiences that help me get through life; by realizing that no matter how bad things appear, I can always look back on them after a period of time and laugh. Boot camp was almost three months long, but it seemed like a lifetime to most of us.

When I arrived home from boot camp, my hometown sweetheart was waiting for me. While I was preparing for the next four years, she was preparing for a lifetime; as my wife. Two days after I hit town we were married in a local church. She had planned it all out. I didn't even get to choose my own best man. It is hard to believe, but that was thirty-three years, three daughters, and one son ago.

Two and one-half weeks after I left boot camp I found myself standing in a massive crowd of people at O'Hare Airport in Chicago. There I was with my sea bag in one hand and my orders to Yokosuka, Japan, in the other. Life was zipping by. A lot had happened over the last six months; I had gone from a small-town high school student, to a factory worker, to a member of the world's largest Navy, to a husband, and now a world traveler. O'Hare is like most big city airports; busy, confusing, and noisy. With so many people all going someplace, this was a new experience for me.

While I was waiting for my plane to Yokosuka, nature called. I began looking for the restroom. For the first time in my life I saw restroom stalls with coin dispensers on each door. I was wearing my Navy dress blues, which had thirteen buttons across the front of the trousers. I had to fish around to find myself a dime to get into the stall. I finally got in and sat on the only seat available. As I was sitting there I noticed that someone had just occupied the stall adjacent to mine. In just a few moments there was a hand extending itself under the wall divider from the other stall. The hand was opening and closing as if it wanted something. It didn't take long for this small-town hick to realize that it was time to get out of Dodge.

I must have looked mighty strange running down the corridor, dragging my sea bag in one hand and trying to button all those buttons with the other. I was beginning to see the world in a different perspective now that I was out in it. I came to the conclusion that if this is what I had been missing by living in a small town all my life, maybe being a country boy wasn't so bad after all.

I finally boarded a 707 for my first airplane ride. Most of the people were extra nice to me, being in uniform and all. One large, older man sat down next to me. He asked, "How long do you think Vietnam is going to last?"

I thought to myself, "How the heck do I know? I don't even know where Vietnam is, and I don't care." I suppose I was getting a little home-sick for the old gang and my new wife.

I was just like thousands of other guys who had their lives turned upside down, and now I was being flown to a place that, two weeks earlier, I didn't know even existed. Have you ever wanted to stop the world and get off for awhile? That is how I was feeling as we were flying across the Pacific Ocean at thirty thousand feet. It also dawned on me that for the next four years, at least, I would have no control over where I would be living, or what I would be doing. I was starting to have my doubts about this military life, with all it's rules and regulations.

We had several stops before our journey would end in Japan. We stopped in San Francisco for a couple of hours; just long enough for me to grab a cab and check out the big city. I had never seen so many hills in all of my life. This was a new and exciting adventure for me. We flew from San Francisco to Hawaii. It was beautiful, like flying over paradise, with it's blue waters, mountains and sandy beaches. Little did I know then that less than a year later I would be back to Pearl Harbor on the Aircraft Carrier, U.S.S. Ranger. We flew from Hawaii to Midway Island, then to Japan.

I arrived in Yokosuka at approximately 1:00 a.m. My orders read that I would be reporting to a RA5C outfit aboard the U.S.S. Ranger. I took a cab from the airport to the Naval Air Station. When I arrived at the main gate, I was told by the military police there to get on board a cattle car. A cattle car was a regular semi-truck and trailer, but the trailer didn't have any walls, just the framework. It was full of sailors, standing or sitting on wooden benches. I jumped on board, sea bag and all.

One of the sailors started talking to me as we pulled out. He told me where to go and how to report in. When the cattle car stopped I went into what appeared to be a large building on the waterfront. There were several jet aircraft in it. I was introduced to one of the fellows in my new outfit. After a little small talk, I said to him, "I thought I was supposed to report to the U.S.S. Ranger. Where is the boat?" He looked at me as if I were crazy, and said, "Man, you've been on her for the last fifteen minutes!"

It was true! I was in the hanger bay of this massive ship. I later learned there were 4,500 officers and men on board, over twice as many people as in my home town. I was told the flight deck stood approximately nine stories out of the water with as much under water. The tallest building in my home-town was the high school, which is only three stories tall.

An hour later I was taken to the berthing area in the forward end of the ship, once I had reported to the petty officer in charge. The bunks were stacked three high, and there was row after row of them. Each bunk had it's own curtain which allowed a fellow to have a little privacy.

SHOCKER AT REVEILLE

I was taken to a corner and given a bottom rack. I learned later that the bottom bunks were for the boot campers and that the top bunks were for the older salts. When I hit the pillow I was out like a light, as it had been a long, lonely day. I was exhausted and homesick.

The next morning, at reveille, I was awakened by the sound of voices. There were several men standing beside my bunk. As I looked out, all I could see was from their knees down. As I crawled out of my bunk one of the men asked me what time I had hit the rack. I told him that it was about 2:00 a.m. He then asked if I had heard the fellow who slept above me get up during the night. I asked him if there was a problem. He told me the nineteen- year- old sailor who slept above me that night had gotten up, gone into the head (bathroom) and hanged himself.

When I had heard that, I was convinced that this Navy life wasn't going to be for me. I wanted to get my sea bag and head back to my home- town where I belonged. I didn't want to be there, and I didn't want to stay, that was for sure!

By noon that day I was assigned a place where I would be working; it was the jet shop. I would be trained to be a jet engine mechanic. Little did I know that before I would leave that squadron, I would have more seniority in that outfit than anyone else. I would see every man in the squadron leave and be replaced by someone new.

Even though I had never seen a jet engine in my life, because of my experience in dad's repair shop back home, they made a jet mechanic out of me. So there I was, a jet engine mechanic. Boy, if the boys back home could see me now! The jet shop was a good place for me. I liked to work with my hands, but I didn't like to get dirty. I thought this would be a good trade to have once I got out of the Navy. I thought that perhaps I could get a job working for some big airline. The jet engines I worked on were capable of pushing an aircraft through the air at Mock two, or twice the speed of sound, 1440 M.P.H.

The jet shop on board ship was a small room about the size of an average bedroom. It had large air ducts coming out of the bulkhead (walls,) leading to other parts of the ship. As I recall, there was only one chair in the entire shop, and that was where the chief petty officer sat; the rest of us sat on boxes or on the metal deck.

There were seventeen men who worked out of the jet shop, nine of which were going to get a divorce the minute we hit stateside. They kept telling me about how worthless their old ladies were, and how all women were just looking for a free meal ticket. After listening to that kind of talk for the next four months, I was beginning to think that perhaps I had made a mistake by getting married. Because we had actually lived together as man and wife for only a week and a half before I left for Japan, I decided I would give it some time.

On my first full day aboard the U.S.S. Ranger, we pulled out to sea. Some of the men I worked with took me up on the flight deck. It was quite a thrill as we were traveling at about 20 knots and heading into the wind. The wind was blowing so hard that we could stand into it at a forty-five degree angle and not fall down. There were several jets on board, and they were tied down with what are called tie-down chains.

The island, near the center and to the right of the flight deck, stood about three stories above the deck. From the island the captain regulated every move that took place on the entire ship.

Little did I know that first day, as I stood gazing up at the island, that one day I would be in the crows-nest with the captain and a Marine escort. I would be disciplined for one of my most deplorable actions.

We were at sea for approximately six hours when we received word that, because of some trouble in the ship's engine room, we were heading back to Yokosuka. It was good news for the troops, because as soon as we anchored it would be party time. When we pulled into port we would hit the beach, as it was called. Everyone was ironing their white uniforms and getting ready for a night out on the town.

Because I had a good amount of money left over from my travel pay to get to Japan, I was invited to go along. They were going to take this boot camper out and show him the ropes. The first time I hit the beach with the boys was quite an experience in the new lifestyle I was thrown into. I went with about ten other guys who were in the same squadron as myself. The first place we went to was a bar by the name of the Cave. It had an entranceway that resembled a cave. As we went in, as I recall, it resembled a cave there also. There were stalactites hanging from the ceiling and stalagmites coming up from the floor.

We located a table large enough for all of us. After awhile I noticed that it seemed as though the place was divided up between sailors and Marines (Jarheads). All of a sudden one of the chief petty officers jumped on the back of a Jarhead and started punching him in the face. Before I realized what was happening, everybody was fisticuffing. I learned one thing that day, if I were to ever get myself into one of these rumbles again, I would tuck in my neckerchief as soon as possible. A neckerchief is that silly necktie that sailors have to wear. One of those Marines grabbed me by my

29

neckerchief and was dragging me around like a rag doll. He was bouncing me off walls, doors, anything and everything that happened to be in the way. Before long the shore patrol showed up and most of us headed for the nearest exit.

It was after this episode that I was accepted by the gang and became "one of the boys." Not long after this incident we pulled out to sea, and all we talked about was the great time we had at the Cave. As I associated with these new friends I realized that this was going to be my lifestyle for the next four years.

The U.S.S. Ranger had a tradition that had been with her since her commission back in 1957. Whenever we had a ship pull up along side of us at sea to take on fuel or supplies, the theme song, "William Tell Overture," would come over the loud speakers. There was a fellow dressed up like the Lone Ranger; he wore a black mask and had two pearl handled six-shooters strapped to his sides. He would mount a life-size plastic white horse that was fastened onto a jeep. He would then be driven up and down the flight deck while the ship was alongside of us and as they departed. I got so sick and tired of hearing that theme song at all hours of the day and night. I still get chills when I hear it today!

Because I didn't meet up with the squadron I was assigned to until about halfway through the cruise, after being aboard ship for four months, we headed stateside. I learned that once we hit the states all the airdales (men in air squadrons) would leave the carrier and go to their home bases. Our home base was in a town about nineteen miles from Orlando, Florida, by the name of Sanford.

It was in Sanford where my wife and I actually had our honeymoon. It felt a little strange when I returned to the states being met by my new bride. We had been married for about five months, but we had actually lived together for less than two weeks. Life wasn't as simple at it was before, because now I had added responsibilities of finding a house, and all the headaches involved.

It was a beautiful marriage. I had the prettiest gal in the whole fleet, and I loved to show her off. As I muse about those days, I often wonder how many of my buddies came around because I was such a likable guy, or because I had a beautiful young wife. I suppose I will never know; perhaps it is better that way.

After a couple of months had passed things began to change. Because I hadn't been in the service long enough to make rank, we were always broke. We had to settle for a tiny eight foot by thirty-six foot mobile home. As if that wasn't bad enough, it sat right in the take-off and landing path of our squadron's Jets, the Vigilante's.

The Vigilante had two jet engines, the J79. The throttle, when they would take off, would be at full bore (after burner) by the time they flew over our cramped little trailer. The noise was so bad that if we didn't cup our ears as they flew over, we would have a headache for hours. We would miss most of our television shows because we couldn't hear them. It was miserable!

My new wife wasn't quite ready for this lifestyle; after all, she was from the same little town in Indiana that I was from. The closest we had come to anything like this was when a 707 would fly over at thirty thousand feet heading for Chicago.

She would sit at home all day in that wee mobile home, listening to that racket (about every twenty minutes on a busy day,) and get depressed. She was homesick, as she missed her dad whom she loved dearly. We were so poor that I would go into gas stations and steal toilet paper and soap.

One day I came home from the base, and we got into an argument. She began throwing things at me and yelling at the top of her lungs, "Get me out of here! Get me out of here!" The honeymoon was over, and reality was setting in. Looking back I realize we should have waited until I made rank before getting married.

We finally moved out of that mobile home and rented a duplex in the country next to some railroad tracks, which was quieter. As I reminisce on those early days of our marriage, I realize it was those days that were instrumental in forming an everlasting bond, having to rely on each other.

After six months of being stateside it was time, once again, to prepare to go to sea. I was ready to go. The bills had overtaken us, and our marriage was starting to be affected by the pressure. Even though I had made some rank over that period of time, it didn't seem to help.

One day, with tears in her eyes, my wife made the announcement that she was going to have a baby. That was the last straw! How could she do this to me? As if things weren't bad enough, she had to get pregnant. I didn't realize, at the time, she was immune to the type of birth control pills she was taking.

So, with a sigh of relief I sent my pregnant wife home to mommy and daddy, and I headed for the Mediterranean Sea.

DING-DONG, THE SOFT SHOE KING

We pulled out of Mayport, Florida, on board the aircraft carrier U.S.S. Saratoga. It was similar to the U.S.S. Ranger. We were informed that the longest we would be at sea, in between ports, would be about two weeks. The Med-cruise, as it was called, was used to demonstrate the American war ships, and we would go from port to port flexing our muscles. We traveled all over the Mediterranean Sea. I saw things that most people only dream about seeing.

One day, after about six months in the Med, we pulled into Naples, Italy. It was going to be a time to relax after working so hard to keep our jets in the air. Our squadron, the Hoot Owls, was going to throw a division party for the troops. Approximately two hours before the party, the jet shop where I worked was informed that we couldn't go to the party until we installed two J79 engines in a Vigilante. Naturally, that didn't do much for the morale of the boys. After about three hours of complaining and belly-aching, we installed the engines.

By the time we finished we had talked ourselves out of going to any blankety-blank Navy party. Half an hour after the engines were mounted, we all were on our way to the party to make up for lost time. When we arrived we noticed that almost everyone there was top-heavy already. We were told that in order to get drinks we had to have tickets. I went to my officer and asked for some. He was snookered and said, "Spread your arms." I spread my arms and he stretched a row of tickets the width of my arms. "There ya go, that should hold you for awhile." We were told that the tickets weren't any good after 11:00 p.m., and it was 10:30 p.m. already. Needless to say, when 11:00 p.m. rolled around all the jet mechanics and myself had at least twenty drinks in front of us.

After an hour we decided to head back to the "Sara". There we were, about ten of us, stumbling down the streets. Some of the guys were relieving themselves on the sidewalk. I am afraid we were poor ambassadors for the good old U.S.A. It is no wonder that we are hated overseas the way we are. One of the boys who came from Philly, by the nickname of Mack the Mech, all of a sudden jumped up on a Volkswagen bug. He was a pretty good size boy, and what a sight as he was jumping up, and down on that car. We all gathered around and cheered on old Mack as he made this spectacle of himself.

There is an old saying, "monkey see, monkey do." As we stumbled down the street I saw this car that had one of those vinyl covers over it. I jumped up on it and commenced doing a little soft- shoe for the boys. The guys all gathered around, clapping their hands and cheering me on. "Go, Ding-Dong, go," they would yell. My nickname was "Ding-Dong Delli." I was a Ding-Dong all right! As I jumped down off the top of this car, someone grabbed my arm from behind. It was the shore patrol accompanied by the air police. One of them informed me that I was going with them. What we didn't realize was that we were just a couple hundred feet from the main gate where we had the party.

The guards put me in a little guard shack that was attached to the main entrance gate. My buddies all started throwing rocks and beer bottles at them, and yelling, "Let's break Ding-Dong out of there!" The military police informed them that if they would leave, then they would let me go. My friends left, but the military police didn't let me go. I was escorted back to the Saratoga where I had to hand over my I.D. and liberty card.

The next day we pulled out to sea. It felt good to be at sea again, with a cool breeze coming off the ocean and the scent of fresh air. I was the talk of the entire squadron, "Good old Ding-Dong sure knows how to have a good time." They called me "Ding-Dong Delli, the Soft-shoe King." After a week had passed I received a letter from the owner of the car I had done my dance on. Come to find out, the car was a brand new Mercedes Benz, and the owner was a Turkish General. This was one of those many times I asked myself, ""How do I get myself into these scrapes?" This Turkish General was demanding I pay two hundred and fifty dollars for the damages done to his Mercedes Benz.

I took the letter to our legal officer, and he informed me that I could take him to court and fight it. I thought to myself, how would that look, a fellow who has been in the service for two years, who did a dance on someone's car? How could I take him to court? It was a miracle that he wasn't taking me to court. I did the only logical thing I felt I could do; I paid for the damages. I had no other recourse but to cash in the savings bonds I had been receiving since the beginning of the cruise. What a mess! I had done it again! It seemed as though life was getting more complicated as I went along.

The fact I had my liberty card taken away, I was informed that the only way I could get it back was to go to Captain's Mass (military court). In the military there is what is called the chain of command. Because I was an Air-dale and a member of a squadron, when I landed into trouble, I would first have to go and see the Executive Officer (second in command) of the squadron. If the charges were severe enough, I would then have to go up the ladder and see the Commanding Officer (first in command) of the squadron. Now if the charges were very serious I would have to climb the ladder even higher to the Executive Officer of the entire Saratoga. If they were going to make me walk the plank for my misconduct, then I would be compelled to go to Captain's Mass. That would be the highest I could go. It was the most dreaded of the masses, and the least that would take place would be a bust in rank.

I was told I would have to go to mass, but to what step no one knew for sure. I was working the night shift from seven to seven on the flight deck. One morning, two weeks later, I hit the rack. I was asleep for one hour when I was awakened out of a sound sleep and was informed that I was going to Mass. A lump immediately formed in my throat as I tremblingly asked, "Which Mass?" The reply was that I was going to bypass the entire chain of command and was going to have to face the captain of the entire ship.

I was terrified. I asked a couple of guys to iron my white uniform and to polish my shoes. I went into the head (bathroom) and tried to shave, but I was so scared that I kept cutting myself. Twenty minutes later I was standing in line with about fifteen other unfortunate chaps; I was the last person in line. We were lined up in the island, on the third deck above the flight deck, just outside of the crow's nest.

One by one men would go into Mass, then ten minutes later come out, most of them with tears in their eyes. I found out later that every one of us had gotten busted. Finally it was my turn to "face the man." I was informed before I entered that I was not to say "yes, sir," or "no, sir, " but to say "yes, Captain," and "no, Captain." As I entered the crow's nest there stood "the man" himself! The captain was standing behind a podium; a rather flimsy looking thing. As I stood before the captain, some jarhead (Marine) screamed at me, "Accused uncover, two!" This was to inform me I was to remove my hat. I never did like those dixie-cup hats we had to wear.

The skipper had always said over the loud speakers time and time again, the things that get people into trouble is not what they put into their mouths, but what comes out. The captain looked me straight in the eyes and asked me what he had said over and over again. I then repeated what I had heard for six months every time we had pulled into port. It was years later I learned the captain had been paraphrasing a verse in the Bible, Matthew 15:11.

The captain then read off the charges against me. I was standing at attention, too frightened to move. Then he said, "I now reduce you to the next inferior pay grade, and sentence you to phase three liberty." Then that infuriating jarhead barked at me again, "Accused cover, two!" That was the command to put my hat back on. Because I was shaking so badly and because I needed a haircut, I had a rough time with my hat. Then the command was given for an "About face." As I turned around I accidentally kicked the podium. Since the captain was still standing behind it, I almost knocked him over.

When I left the crow's nest I was instructed to stand at attention. One of the Marines went back into the crow's nest and retrieved the podium. I was then told to carry it. So off we went, down five or six ladders (stairs) into the hangar bay. As I was walking with the podium over my shoulder, with a Marine on each side of me, someone yelled out, "Look, it's Jesus Christ!" I continued with the podium over my shoulder until we went about four decks below water level to where the podium was stowed. After that, I was escorted to the barber- shop. There were about fifty men standing in line for a haircut, because we were pulling into port in a few days. That day I received head of the line privileges. I sat down, and three minutes later when I got up I was completely bald.

I was depressed, to say the least, and sorry I had put myself into this mess. After a few days I learned what phase three liberty was. I could only leave the ship on the thirtieth day from my sentence, if we happened to be in port. If not, I would have to wait another thirty days from that date, and so on, and so on. Not only could I not leave the ship, except on the thirtieth day, but when I did leave I had to have an E4 petty officer, or above, sign me out and baby sit me.

It was worse than being in jail. Every time we pulled into port all the boys would have to tell me what a great time I had missed. Finally, three months later, on the ninetieth day from my Captain's Mass, we were in Athens, Greece. I had a good friend from Texas by the name of Larry Gene Kielberg who I talked into signing me out. We all called Larry Gene the "Doc" because he was so witty. We went down to the master-at-arms headquarters where he was going to sign me out. When we arrived we were told that if either of us got into trouble while we were on the beach they would hang the both of us. I told Larry Gene that all I wanted to do was to take a tour, or just look around a bit, anything, just get me off the ship!

When we went down the gangplank and I stepped on solid ground, I knelt down and kissed the earth. We headed for beautiful downtown Athens and, of course, the first bar we came to we entered.

Every time we pulled into port the chaplain would make an announcement on ship T.V. of all the places that were off limits to all military personnel. Almost always everyone would go to those places because there weren't any military police in those areas. After being in the bar for an hour or so we met one of the natives of Athens. He told us about a wine festival that was going on the other side of town. Larry Gene said, "Wasn't that one of the places the chaplain said was off limits?" A big smile came over both of our faces as we paid our bill and went out and flagged down a taxi. We reasoned with each other, surely we wouldn't get into any trouble because there wouldn't be any shore patrol for miles around that place.

It was almost dark when we arrived and, just as we had suspected, half the fleet was there. As we entered the festival, we were given a plastic cup and pitcher. The festival site was in the hills overlooking Athens. It was in a wooded area and resembled any big city park in the United States. Amongst the trees were barrels of wine resting on their sides on little stands. Each barrel had it's own spigot, and we were allowed to take as much wine as we wanted.

In each of the four- corners of the festival there was a musical band and a huge wooden wine vat. In each vat there were women crushing grapes with their bare feet. As they crushed the grapes the juice would run down into a large wooden bucket. It was a sight to behold, especially after being locked up on the Saratoga for the last ninety days.

It was a hot summer day and we were wearing our dress white uniforms. As we were walking down one of the paths we were approached by two, black American sailors from a destroyer. As we passed each other, one of them threw his pitcher of red wine all over Larry Gene's dress white uniform.

Larry Gene's response was to ask, "What in the blankety-blank is wrong with you dude?"

To our surprise he looked Larry Gene in the eye and said, "Why do you white trash want to discriminate against the Negro?" I couldn't believe my ears! He had just drenched the "Doc" with wine, and he wanted to know why we wanted to discriminate against the Negro! The "Doc" took his stance as if to go into battle, two of them, and two of us.

As we stood there about to go at each other's throats, it dawned on me what the master-at-arms told us on the Saratoga. If one of us got into trouble we both would be held accountable. I sure didn't want to be restricted to the ship again! Somehow, I talked the "Doc" into forgetting about what had just happened, and we started to leave. About that time there were about three or four more of them coming out of the bushes with blades flashing from off the lights from above. Needless to say, the "Doc" and I ran for our lives, out of the festival and down the street toward Athens.

We ran to a street corner where we caught our breath, and were waiting to flag down a cab, when a fellow whom I took to be from Athens, walked over to Larry Gene and asked him for a cigarette. The "Doc" didn't smoke, so I bent over to get my cigarettes out of my sock (all cool sailors carried their smokes I their socks,) and as I did so this jerk coughed up a big lunger and spit it into the "Doc's" face. That was the last straw! Larry Gene grabbed him by the throat and was choking him to death. I grabbed Larry Gene, jumped in front of an oncoming cab, threw him into it, and headed back to the Saratoga. When we finally arrived Larry Gene said, "Don't you ever ask me to baby-sit you again. You're trouble!"

We were at sea for about two weeks when I received a letter from my father-in-law informing me that I was the father of a fine baby girl, Lori Marie. It would be at least four months before I would see her for the first time.

NAVY LIFE

Life on an aircraft carrier can be hectic at times. Our squadron had only six aircraft, but it was a real challenge trying to keep them airworthy all the time. One of the things that discouraged me most, while I was in the Navy, was standing in lines for everything. Sometimes we would have to stand in line for an hour or more just to eat. There were two galleys, one in the aft part of the ship where normal meals were served (for the most part good food). Near the bow of the ship the second galley was open twenty-four hours a day; where all they served most of the time was hot dogs and beans. This galley was for those who were too busy to stand in line for long periods of time.

Each carrier has it's own T.V. station and radio station. Once I called my wife from the middle of the ocean by way of C.B. radio. The C.B. operator located someone in Connecticut who then called from his phone to Indiana. Even though we were thousands of miles apart we were only charged for the call from Connecticut to Indiana.

There are stores aboard ship where one can buy clothes, stores for candy and ice cream, and stores for entertainment. The ship had it's own laundry, post office, library, and anything else a small town would have.

When we did a lot of flying, we would sometimes use up all the fresh water in the steam-driven catapults. The catapults were the mechanisms that flung the aircraft off the flight deck. When this happened we would go on what is called "water hours." During this time fresh water would be turned on only at certain times of the day. If one was going to shower, that would be the time to do so.

Time went by quickly while we were busy flying, but when we stopped the time dragged by. On day, during a time when we weren't flying, they had what is referred to as a "smoker" in the hangar bay. A "smoker' is when all the best boxers from all the ships in the fleet would come on board and fight our best boxers. I had never witnessed anything like it. The grand finale was when they put fifteen men in the ring at the same time. They had one hand tied behind their back and were blindfolded. When the bell rang it was every man for himself. A boxer was eliminated when he hit the deck. Along the outside of the ring there were men with broomsticks with boxing gloves taped to one end. They would prod the men, thus provoking them to swing back. The winner received a gold watch.

In my spare time I took karate lessons. I learned just enough karate, that if I tried to use it, I would undoubtedly get beat to death.

Approximately three and one half months after I received word that I was a father, word was passed that we were heading stateside. It had been a long, frustrating cruise for me, being in trouble the way I had been. It would be nice to be home again with my wife and new daughter. By this time all our bills had been paid, and Margie had bought us a nice looking 1966 Chevy. We even had some money in the bank. I found out that it is almost impossible to spend all of ones money while at sea.

We were almost halfway home when we ran into a storm. I had never seen such a storm in my life. I had to strap myself into my rack at night. The storm lasted for about a week. The waves were so huge that they were coming over the flight deck, which is almost ninety feet off the water. When we went down to the galley the ship would sway so badly our tray would slide over to the guy next to us. The fellow sitting next to me, his tray slid over in front of me. It was a good thing I liked what was on the trays of the men on each side of me.

We had at least two destroyers escorting us at all times. When I went up on the flight deck and looked out for those destroyers, they looked like submarines. All around the flight deck is what is called the "catwalk." The catwalk is a metal walkway that is about four feet below the flight deck. When the storm was finally over, those catwalks in the forward section of the ship looked like a banana peel.

We were two days late dropping anchor stateside. It was sure good to be back home. My wife, and baby daughter, had arrived three days earlier and were waiting for me. Our home base had been relocated from Sanford, Florida to Albany, Georgia. The base in Albany had been an Air Force base.

When we first arrived in town there were signs all over town welcoming us to their community. What the people of Albany didn't realize was that we flew our noisy jets day and night. The Air Force, for the most part, flew only during the daytime, and their aircraft didn't have jet engines. Our pilots had to practice landing on a simulated flight deck around the clock. After six months of all that noise, all the "welcome Navy" signs came down. There were even incidents of farmers shooting at our planes.

We moved into a quiet little mobile home park about three miles out of town. By this time I had made some rank and was now a third class petty officer, and we were able to make ends meet. After being at sea all those months, and working twelve hours a day, it felt good to work an eight- hour day. Things were going well for us. I would never admit it then, but I was beginning to enjoy the title "jet engine mechanic." We bought all our food at the commissary and went to the Navy doctors. It was a standing joke with some of the Navy doctors that no matter what you sent your wife to the doctor for, his first request was for her to strip down to the waist. If they went in for a migraine headache, it was strip to the waist. If they went in with a stiff neck, it was strip to the waist. In the military you do it their way or you go someplace else. When I learned what was taking place I stopped my wife from going to the doctor on the base, and we started going someplace else.

Most of the men I had been on board ship with talked like typical sailors at sea, but when we hit stateside most of us tried to watch our language around our wives. I am ashamed to admit that I had picked up some bad habits while being in the service, most of which have taken years to correct. Even now, after twenty-five years, I still have flashbacks of the old days.

THE LONE RANGER RIDES AGAIN

My last cruise would be spent on the U.S.S. Ranger. I had been on her before, straight off of boot camp leave. So, we were off to California again. When we arrived at the Ranger we were assigned different work and berthing areas than last time. What I dreaded most about this whole cruise was listening to the theme song from the Lone Ranger for the next nine months.

By this time I had become an old-timer in the squadron as over half of the original guys I had signed up with had gotten out or transferred to other units. I was an old "salt," I knew my way around the Ranger pretty well.

I ran into an old high school buddy of mine one day while I was down in the galley. He was ships' company and lived on the Ranger while we were in the states. He was what is referred to as a "snip," because he worked on the boilers of the ship. He took me deep into the bottom of the ship; it was rather frightening. An airdale didn't have any business below the hangar bay. Somehow I felt a little better about this cruise knowing that I had an old buddy on board with me.

Our berthing area was at the aft end of the ship, directly under the flight deck. It was located under the cables that are stretched across the deck to stop the jets as they land. As I was in a top bunk I could literally, from lying on my back, touch the bottom side of the flight deck. It wasn't until we went out to sea, and started flying, that I realized that this was one of the most dangerous places to be, and one of the noisiest!

Many of the jets would return to the carrier with bombs still on them. If they were to miss the flight deck it would kill everyone in our berthing area. Only a few months prior, that very thing happened on a carrier off the coast of Vietnam, where we were at this time.

The first time I was in my rack and a jet landed, it sounded as though someone had taken a sledge hammer right over my rack and hit the flight deck as hard as they could. It was terrible; I had nine months of this to look forward to, plus the Lone Ranger theme song!

When an aircraft would approach the carrier, a large steel hook would be dropped from the tail end of it. The idea of this was for the pilot to grab hold of the cable with the hook. As the cable would stretch out, the tension would increase, thus enabling the aircraft to stop.

I didn't get a complete night's sleep for months. I had to resort to wearing earplugs to bed. I almost always had a headache upon arising. It wasn't until almost halfway through the cruise that I realized I was going to have to get accustomed to that sledge hammer noise, or lose a lot of sleep. I could hear the aircraft approaching the carrier, so I would always cover my head with my pillow, even in my sleep!

Being one of the old "salts," and familiar with the flight deck activity, I was placed on night shift from seven to seven, and worked on the flight deck. It was extremely dangerous; we had propeller driven {spads} aircraft on board, along with jets. When a jet would be "turning up," the noise would be so loud that one couldn't hear anything else. If we, on the flight deck, weren't very careful we could walk into a spinning propeller and kill ourselves.

45

While we were in the combat zone off the coast of Vietnam, we would have "lights out" on the flight deck a large part of the time. We had to use a red lens in our flashlights so as not to be seen from shore. All the aircraft were armed with bombs and missiles, some of them weighing from five hundred pounds to one ton. I had a special clearance enabling me to assist in loading these bombs on phantom jets. When I stop and think about it, we were on a gigantic ammunition depot, with thousands of tons of bombs and missiles. Many of the jets would leave the carrier fully loaded with bombs and missiles, and half an hour later return empty. I often wondered about how many people were killed by the planes leaving the Ranger.

Once, we had two of our aircraft shot down near Da Nang, South Vietnam. There were four of us who volunteered to go in to fix them and get them airworthy again. We were loaded on what is called a mail C.O.D., a propeller driven aircraft with two engines. The mail C.O.D. was hooked up to the catapult, a steam driven device that would actually fling the aircraft off the flight deck. What a thrill it was as the engines revved up, and the catapult flung us off the flight deck! The G-force slammed us back into our seats. After takeoff, it is common for the aircraft to drop below the flight deck level for a few moments. All we could see was water.

I have had some anxious moments as I would often stard on the flight deck watching our aircraft being launched. When it would drop below the flight deck level, I was never sure it would rise again.

It was time to relax a little as we were climbing into the clouds. Gazing out the window, I saw a very small ship in a very big ocean. It was hard to believe that aircraft could land on that carrier, looking down on her from this height. It was also hard to believe that there were 4,500 officers and men on board her.

We eventually started flying over land, heading for Da Nang. I glanced out the window, only to see great white puffs of smoke; we had encountered an assault from the jungle below. Those were uneasy moments, to say the least. When we landed in Da Nang, we were issued army green uniforms and a rifle. To be honest, I didn't know how to load the rifle even if

I had to. We went in to retrieve one of two planes that had gone down weeks earlier.

At that time, Da Nang was the busiest airport in the world, with a plane either landing or taking off every three minutes. We had to convert two jet engines out of Marine Phantom jets to make them fit into our Vigilante. This was the end of 1968, and we would be there until 1969.

When we had been there for awhile, we made up our minds that we were going to go to the commissary and buy some hero stuff; jungle hats, camouflaged pants, and whatever we could send back home. The next morning we were informed the commissary had been bombed during the night and no longer existed. We were warned, before leaving the ship, not to go to the top floor of a barracks, because when a raid was made and bombs dropped, the shrapnel would destroy the top deck first.

Early one morning, around three o'clock, I awakened and saw my chief petty officer sitting on the edge of his bunk, smoking one cigarette after another. He looked over at me and said, "Ding Dong, I knew this would happen; I've got only six months before I retire and I'm going to die in this hell-hole." Poor guy, all he could think about was that some slob would be living off his benefits with his wife. It then dawned on me, this was a real war we were involved in; people were being killed every day.

Not long after we had finished our mission in Da Nang, we were flown to Subic Bay in the Philippine Islands. Before we had left Vietnam word was passed to me that I had passed my rating test and was advanced to E-5, second class petty officer. When we finally arrived at Subic Bay, the U.S.S. Ranger looked like the Hilton compared to where we had been.

A strange thing happened, after I made second class, that I hadn't anticipated; the old gang changed toward me. Making rank meant taking on more responsibilities, including the fact that some of the guys were working for me, not just with me. It reminded me about the time when I had become a senior in high school and captain of the basketball team. I was no longer a junior with all my expectations ahead of me. Funny how that happens a lot in life as we mature and accept the responsibilities along the way.

The cruise on the U.S.S. Ranger was a lengthy one. I knew this would, no doubt, be my last cruise, and I was anxious to get it over. After I had been discharged from the Navy, I would have a dream. It went like this: I would be at home with my wife and daughter, the phone would ring, and it would be my chief. He would tell me to pack my sea bag. I had one more cruise to make. I would wake up then and realize that I would never go to sea again, thank God!

The day finally came when word was passed that we were going to be heading stateside. Within two weeks we were in California on board a military transport, heading for Albany, Georgia.

When my wife and daughter had moved back down from Indiana and we were settled in, it was just a matter of time until I would receive my discharge date. I was assigned to the base jet shop where we performed all the major repair work for the entire base. Being an E-5 I didn't have very much to do. Each day we would play volleyball for a couple of hours. I would take a couple of hours off for lunch, and would often leave work early.

One day I was approached by the maintenance officer, who asked me to go to his office, he asked me how I liked the jet shop, and if I would like to stay in the Navy for another four years. He said there would be a large bonus, and I wouldn't have to go to sea for at least four years. It sounded pretty good for about five minutes; then I remembered all the lonely watches I had stood, and all the trouble I had been in while overseas, plus all the time away from my little family. I had too many plans for the future, and myself, and my family. It was like being a junior in high school again with all the dreams and hopes for the future. So, on November 7, 1969, after receiving a ninety day early out, I was honorably discharged from the world's largest Navy.

HOPES AND DREAMS FOR THE FUTURE

One of my dreams, after being discharged from the Navy, was to become a licensed aircraft mechanic with the F.A.A. One of the best aeronautical schools in America is found in Daytona Beach, Florida. I was determined to go and take advantage of the four years jet engine mechanic experience I had while in the Navy. I had been discharged in Albany, Georgia, so I had the Navy ship all our belongings to Daytona Beach and store it there.

Meanwhile, my wife and daughter and I moved back to Indiana. I went back to work at my old job that I had taken a leave of absence from when I went into the Navy, the Ford Motor Company in Chicago Heights, Illinois. Because I had gone into the service while being employed there, all my service time counted as seniority. The pay was really good, and with almost four and one half years seniority I could work any shift I chose. The reason I had all our belongings shipped to Daytona Beach was to insure my going there to school and not talking myself out of it. I stayed just long enough at the Ford Motor Company to acquire all of my vacation pay, visit our folks for awhile, and then it was off to aircraft mechanics school.

We arrived in Daytona Beach approximately one month before I would start classes. I began searching for a job. We rented a little one- bedroom shack and picked up our belongings from the storage.

The first job I hired into was at a steak house. I was told to come in early and I could have a free meal. After I had eaten, some of the guys took me back to the kitchen and left me to figure things out for myself. Finally, after about half an hour, I was told to go out behind the counter. By this time the place was packed with customers. It felt as though everyone was staring at me. It was my job to make Texas toast, and to cut a baked potato in half and put a scoop of butter in it. Things were going along fairly well for about ten minutes, even though I had butter all over me and the floor. I was slipping and sliding all over the place. Then to my chagrin I ran out of spuds! I didn't know that when I took a baked potato out of the oven I was supposed to replace it with another one. After awhile the customers started complaining to my boss and pointing at me. Well, that was my first and last day at the steak house. I told my wife that I would go back in the Navy before I would go through that again!

The next day I went out looking for another source of employment. This time I found a job at a recap tire shop. That was a little more down my alley, and I stayed there until I graduated two years later. I received an airframes and power plants license, better known as an A/P certificate. This made me legal to work on anything that flew. Again, this was a time in my life when I had big plans, hopes, and dreams of making it big in the aviation industry.

A few months before graduation we learned that Margie was going to have our second child. So, I headed out to set the aviation industry on fire. I believed that with all my military experience, and now an A/P license I wouldn't have any problem finding an excellent job. I purchased myself a new suit, got a haircut and put some polish on my shoes. I heard through the grapevine that they were hiring A/P mechanics in Lake City, Florida, so away I went! When I had my job interview, the interviewer was wearing a pair of bib overalls and a white tee shirt. He looked at me real hard and then told me I looked more like a Bible salesman than a mechanic. I didn't tell him what I thought he looked like! He asked, "How do I know you can work out of a tool box?" I replied, "That's simple, hire me and find out."

As I look back on those days I realize I had an attitude problem. My first job was to work on Marine cargo planes, the Hercules, the type where the tail section drops down and jeeps can be driven into it. This job took a little wind out of my sails, as I installed the "honey buckets" (bathroom commodes) in each aircraft. I was later known as "the honey bucket king," thus bruising my ego. Most of the people I worked with didn't have any military experience or a high school diploma.

Every shop has employees who knew somebody that knew somebody. Because it was a military contract, they had to hire some of the locals. My boss was one of the good old boys. His name was Broderick Pine. I had misunderstood his name, and called him Mr. Broderick; unbeknownst to me, this irritated him to no end. Like most of the good old boys, he didn't take a liking to Yankees anyhow.

One day I was to install a dozen bolts in the cargo floor of the Hercules. I was working with a young, single fellow by the name of Ron. He was supposed to go under the aircraft and put nuts on these three- foot long bolts, and I was going to tighten them from the cargo area. Ron left the cargo area and became sidetracked along the way; there were a large number of women working there. So, there I sat with a wrench in my hand, waiting for Ron to rap on the bottom of the plane signaling to me that I could tighten those bolts. Along about this time Broderick Pine came into the plane (it was about one hundred and twenty degrees in the cargo area) and asked me what in the blankety-blank did I think I was doing? I explained to him that I was installing these three- foot long bolts through the cargo area floor, and that I was waiting for Ron to rap on the bottom of the plane.

Five minutes later Mr. Pine returned and asked me what in the blankety-blank I was doing sitting there, doing nothing. Looking up from my sitting position I said, "Mr. Broderick, I told you once, but this time I will go real slow so you can get it all." When I called him Mr. Broderick some of the women in the cargo area started laughing at him. This made him even angrier than before.

He said, "I ought to write you up," and stomped off. Just about that time Ron stuck his head into the plane and said, "I've got to go to the restroom, I'll be back in a minute."

Sure enough, here came Broderick Pine. He looked down at me, the perspiration running off his face by this time, and said "That's it, I'm going to write you up." I looked up at him and replied, "Mr. Broderick, you can take this job and this plane and shove them up your nose sideways."

By this time the poor fellow was jumping up and down, yelling at the top of his lungs, "Insubordination, insubordination! You're fired, you're fired!" I had a quick temper back in those days, and it took all I had to keep from decking him.

Fifteen minutes later I was standing outside the gate looking in, with my tool box in one hand, and my termination papers in the other. As I was driving home to my very pregnant wife, I was trying to think of something intelligent to tell her, but the words never came. How did I get myself into these jams?

As I pulled into the driveway I could tell by the look on my wife's face that she knew something was amiss. There I was with a pregnant wife, no job, no insurance, and no hope. The next day I went out to find another job. Three days later I got a job in St. Augustine, Florida. I would still be working in the aircraft business, but the problem was it was about one hundred and thirty miles away. The aircraft manufacturer I would be working for had a military contract to build test planes for the Air Force. Because Margie was eight and one half months along in her pregnancy, no other doctor would take her as a patient, and besides, we didn't have any insurance. We already had the doctor paid in Lake City. So, we moved to Jacksonville to split the difference in distance.

After I was on the job for awhile I started commuting with a fellow worker. We alternated weeks. It was a real hassle living in Jacksonville and Margie having to go to the doctor in Lake City. I even left her in Lake City with my brother and his family for awhile, but then I'm getting ahead of myself.

As I was driving to work one day, this lady decided she was going to cross the freeway. She was driving an older brown station wagon. I ran into the passenger side of her car so hard that the passenger side door was wrapped around the steering wheel. We were all rushed to the emergency room in a nearby hospital in an ambulance. Luckily, no one was seriously injured, only cuts and bruises. Both vehicles were totaled because of the speed I had been traveling. The accident took place on a Friday, and the next day Jim came over and said that he would like to talk to me. After the usual small talk he informed me that he was going to sue me for fifty thousand dollars, because of the injuries done to him in the accident. I couldn't believe my ears! I told him that if he did that my insurance rate would go up for the rest of my life. He then said that we would split the fifty thousand, fifty-fifty. I finally talked him out of it after about an hour, and he went home. After totaling out my car I borrowed one and took Margie to my brother's house in Lake City, because I was afraid she would go into labor while we were without a car and I would be unable to take her the sixty miles to the hospital in Lake City. After Jim had gone home I called Margie and told her the whole story. She had a big laugh over the whole thing.

The following Monday I woke up at the regular time to go to work, expecting Jim to come by and pick me up. When he hadn't arrived by an hour and one half later, I decided to hitch hike to work some thirty miles away as Jim didn't have a telephone I couldn't call him. I was quite late for work, but I went straight to Jim's work area, as I had a bone to pick with him. He wasn't there; as a matter of fact, he didn't show up at all that day. Needless to say, I made new arrangements for getting to and from work. I had been home from work approximately one hour when Jim's wife called asking for Jim. I told her that not only was he not there, but he never showed up for work either! Four or five hours later she called again saying she still hadn't heard from Jim. No one heard from Jim again, not his wife, not his four children, not at work, not me, no one! The way I figure, Jim got up Monday and headed for work, and just kept on going. We've all felt that way from time to time, especially on a Monday morning. This was one fellow who lived out his fantasy.

Jim was like many of us, wanting to run away from our responsibilities and obligations of life. Some people did it with drugs, alcohol, and sex, anything to make an escape from reality. The truth of the matter is, you can run but you can't hide. If we run far enough away, it will just take longer to catch up with us, but sooner or later we will be found. About two weeks after all this happened, Margie gave birth to our second daughter, Marla Ann.

If my memory serves me correctly, I had about nine jobs that first year out of aircraft mechanics school, two from which I was fired. Most of the places I worked had military contracts, one was a flight school, and one an aircraft repair station. In those days I would quit a job at a drop of a hat and go to another one, always looking for more money, more benefits, or a little security.

I began to feel like I had my senior year in high school, with all the pressures on me, and no more dreams and big plans to look forward to. I didn't like that feeling. Maybe this aviation business wasn't what it was all cracked up to be.

After two years in aviation, I decided to try something else. So, through the G.I Bill I went into the carpentry trade; I went to school two nights a week and worked as a carpenter's apprentice during the day. I thought I would like carpentry, but I would have to go down to the union hall for days at a time and wait for a job. The pressure of the bills was making life very uncomfortable, especially with a wife and two kids.

One day I got hooked up with a carpenter, who was called "Ronchy," who was well known in the Jacksonville area as being an ace carpenter.

"Ronchy" took me under his wing and showed me the ropes, but the trouble was, he was in jail more than he was out. We wouldn't do much work, but we sure did have a good time. After some pretty lean paychecks, I decided to go back into aviation. To me life was meaningless, I felt like I was spinning my wheels and getting nothing accomplished. It seemed as though I was going from one rotten job to another, and to be honest, life was beginning to reek. I often thought about what Jim had done and thought, maybe that would help in my situation!

SECURITY AT LAST

One summer day we had visitors, my wife's sister, Jean, and her husband, Dan, who had driven down from Indiana. They were driving a new car and had just remodeled their home, and their four children were all dressed in new clothes. I asked Dan, "Man, what do you do for a living?" He told me he shined plows at one of the local factories. He was on piecework and was making three times more money than I was as an aircraft mechanic.

Here I was beating my brains out, working two jobs, and I couldn't even afford to pay the rent. I had all the responsibilities of a licensed mechanic, and was getting paid gas station attendant wages. It didn't make any sense. I always did say that in America the harder one works, the less one makes. If you doubt what I am saying, then the next time you are driving down a road that is under construction, ask that young gal with a flag in her hand how much money per hour is she making.

I told Dan to send me an application from the place he was working when he got back home. About two weeks after they left to go back home I received an application. I filled it out immediately and sent it back to Dan.

Three weeks later we packed up all we had, which wasn't much, and headed North. We arrived in Indiana in July of 1972, and the following month I began working at Allis-Chalmers.

After a year on the assembly line, because of my background in mainte-nance, I was put into the pipe shop as a pipe fitter. Six months later all the other pipe fitters had retired, leaving me with top seniority in the pipe shop. That meant that, not only would I make top pay, I would never get laid off. After six years of my jumping from one bad job to another. Of a life of worrying about us getting our gas and electric shut off. Receiving threaten-ing mail about our being turned over to a collection agency. Never having money to do the things we wanted. I had finally had gotten a good job!

Things were now going to be different for us. We bought our first house, a cute, little two bedroom in a little town five miles from where I worked. One of the things I liked about our new home was that it was a stone's throw from a bar. I would jokingly say I could always crawl home from there if I had to, and I had to on more than one occasion.

Although it seemed as if we had finally gotten it together, with a good job and a new home, our marriage was on the rocks. My drinking and hanging out with the guys was driving us apart. I can remember when my mother-in-law came over, she had gone to the refrigerator for something and the only thing in it was a case of Budweiser. She began preaching to me. I told her that when she started paying the bills around there she could then tell me what I could have, or not have, in my refrigerator.

I used to tell my wife the only reason I didn't divorce her was because I couldn't afford it. This went on for months, and then one Saturday after-noon as I was watching a ball game on T.V. a car pulled up in front of the house. This dude had on a suit and tie, so I thought it was a holy- roller from down the street. I thought to myself, I'll get rid of this jerk in a hurry. When I answered the door he asked for me by name. When I told him who I was he told me that my wife had filed for divorce and handed me some papers. He then informed me that I had twenty minutes to vacate the pre-mises. He asked Margie if she would like for him to stay while I gathered my things together; she told him no, and he left. I couldn't believe what was happening as I stood there with a set of divorce papers in my hands. Meanwhile, Margie ran into the bathroom and barricaded herself in and me out.

I threw a fit and started yelling and cursing. Then I commenced smashing furniture, lamps, pictures, and anything that got in my way. I tried kicking in the bathroom door, to no avail. I went to the refrigerator and got out a six pack of Bud and sat down outside of the bathroom door on the floor. I was going to get even with that woman if it took all night!

The first thing I realized when I woke up the next morning was that Margie had slipped out and taken my two daughters with her. I gathered all my clothes and checked into a hotel in town. The place was roach infested and stank to high heaven. I thought to myself, "So, this is the thanks I get for putting up with 'that woman' for all these years!"

Several months earlier Margie had gotten a job at the same factory where I worked. We both were on the night shift and it seemed as though we were always running into each other. Finally, about a month after we had separated, I asked her if we could get together after work and talk things over. She was quite reluctant at first, but finally gave in to my request.

The first place we went to was the nearest bar, but just like always, Margie wouldn't go in, so I went in and bought a six pack of beer. We talked for hours. Neither one of us really wanted a divorce, but we both knew our marriage wouldn't work out the way things were going. I made Margie all kinds of promises that I never had any intention of keeping, and I moved back home. I tried to prove my love for her by buying her things. I found myself spending money I didn't have to buy things we didn't need to impress people I didn't like. It was the old "keep up with the Jones'" routine. When the bills started rolling in, the pressure came with them, and then tension in the home. It was like a vicious circle.

We purchased a beautiful, four- bedroom, cape-cod home in a new subdivision on the edge of town. It looked like a dream home from the outside, but our marriage was a nightmare on the inside. After I had worked my eight- hour shift I clocked out and then would go back to the shop and spend an hour or so with the guys. I hated to go home because my wife and I were always at each other's throats.

I came to the conclusion that I should get involved in some kind of a project, and then maybe things would be different at home. I had seen an ad in a flying magazine that said, "Fly for only two hundred dollars." I sent away for a set of blueprints on how to build a glider. My first trip to the lumberyard cost over two hundred and fifty dollars, and that was just for the lumber. I knew then, it was going to cost about five hundred dollars for this project that was supposed to keep me out of trouble for awhile. When I had finished it, it resembled the Wright Brothers first airplane.

The glider had two wings, each one twenty eight feet long, and the tail section was fifteen feet deep. In order to get it airborne we would tow it, and I would ride it from a harness near the very front of the plane.

One day we were towing it from the back of a pickup truck. The idea was, once I was airborne they would throw the tow- rope out of the truck, and the truck would then speed up so I wouldn't land on it. I was about sixty feet in the air and they threw the rope out of the truck. The truck then sped up, but somehow the rope got tangled up on the truck's bumper. When the truck sped up it jerked me skyward, at first, then straight down.

After the crash, I could barely walk because of the impact. The glider had broken in two pieces across my back. I was in pain for weeks, but I was too proud to go to the doctor. It didn't take very long for me to get rid of that project and start looking for something closer to the ground to occupy my spare time.

A couple weeks later I was talking to a brother-in-law of mine at work. He was several years older than me, and was into jogging. His brother, Ralph, who was also into jogging, was a perfect specimen of a man. He worked hard all day shining plows, and then after he got home at the end of the day he would jog for ten miles every day. He invited me over to his home and showed me all his trophies, of which there was quite a collection, from all the races he had won. He challenged me that I couldn't run for three miles without stopping. I thought to myself, "If this old man can do it, so can I."

A few days later I bought myself a pair of jogging shoes and a set of sweats. I figured out how far three miles was from the odometer on my car. It was a cold November day, and it had just rained. I told myself that I would run a mile and a half out, and then a mile and a half back. I took off like a blaze, but after about a half mile out my side developed a pain, and then about the one-mile mark my head started hurting. By the time I hit the turn around point, I had to stop and upchuck my dinner I had eaten only half an hour before I had started running.

I didn't tell Ralph until months later that I had failed miserably on my first attempt as a jogger. I had been out of school for about ten years and was out of shape, to say the least. As time went on, Ralph asked me to join him, my brother-in-law Dan, and a couple doctors from the area, to run in competition with them.

By that time I could run for ten miles without stopping and was going pretty good. We traveled all over Indiana and Michigan, participating in races. Before I had retired from jogging I had run in two marathons (twenty-six mile races) and had averaged over one hundred miles per week. Even after all that practicing and running, the closest I ever came to beating Ralph in a race was five seconds.

All these activities I was involved in didn't help our marriage. We didn't see very much of each other, and I still drank and smoked and went out with the guys, trying to find something to fill the void I had in my life.

My next activity was golfing. Naturally, I went out and bought the best set of clubs, shoes, and of course, hat and gloves. I looked like a golfer, talked like a golfer, drank my beer with the golfers, but the truth of the matter was, I wasn't a golfer!

It wasn't long after that I started looking for something else to fill the void that was haunting my life. I often thought, "There has to be more to life than working, making bills, then working to pay them off. If you gather too much in a lifetime, the kids will be at each other's throats fighting over what you left behind after you drop dead, so what's the use?"

My children had all the latest toys, and the finest clothes that money could buy. One would have thought that we had the world by the tail. What people didn't know was that about every weekend I would run down to the credit union and get out a couple hundred bucks just for the weekend. I figured it wasn't a big deal; I had the next thirty years to pay it off. Life was still miserable and unsatisfying, and besides all that, I was up to my eyeballs in debt. In short, life stunk!

FROM THE KING OF BEERS TO THE KING OF KINGS

One Sunday morning, I believe it was the second week in October, something happened that would eventually change my life and eternal destiny. I was sitting in our living room having a cup of hot, black coffee, trying to alleviate a splitting headache from the night before. As I looked out our large bay window to the street, I saw an old blue and white bus pull up to the curb. The driver blew the horn and a whole bunch of kids in the neighborhood ran to climb aboard, and off to Sunday school they went.

I called my wife over and said, "See that bus going down the street? Next Sunday you get up bright and early, dress those noisy kids of yours, and put them on that bus." I figured that with the kids out of the house I could sleep until noon. Sure enough, the next Sunday Margie got up early and put those noisy kids of hers on that blue and white bus.

I didn't know where the church was, what kind it was, or who the pastor was; furthermore I couldn't care less. I woke up around noon, the kids were still gone, and it was so peaceful and quiet. I thought to myself, "What a service – free babysitting." I didn't know there was such a thing like that in town. I wondered why no one at work told me about it. After all, a little religion wouldn't hurt those little heathens anyway.

Things were working out pretty well with this new babysitting service. Every Sunday my wife would get up and put the kids on that bus, and every Sunday I would sleep until about noon.

After about a month of this, on a Thursday night, I was sitting in our new home watching T.V. I had learned a little trick while in the Navy; I would get a six pack of beer out of the refrigerator and feel like I had accomplished a victory if I could get to the sixth can before the chill was gone. I was on my third can when a car pulled up in the driveway. A fellow got out wearing a suit and tie. The last dude who came to my door wearing a suit served me with divorce papers! As I watched, I noticed there was a woman with him. As I lit up a Winston I asked my wife, "Who the blankety-blank is that?"

I must have been a little discourteous when I answered the door and asked, "What do you want?" because the lady took a step backward. The man stood his ground as he stated that he was the pastor of the church we had been sending our kids to, and that the lady was his wife. I turned to look at my wife, expecting her to run and lock herself in the bathroom again.

I thought to myself, "And now they want a donation or something." I knew this free babysitting was too good to be true. I invited them in, and as I sat down I hid the last three cans of Bud alongside the couch. We talked about our kids, our beautiful new home, my job, and then came the subject of religion. I told him that my mother-in-law had enough religion for all of us.

As quick as they got on the subject, I was just as quick to get off the subject. Their church building was being built on the edge of town on a three- acre parcel of land. The preacher-man asked me if I knew anything about the building trade. For the next half- hour I bragged on myself. I told him I could build anything; I was a carpenter, a plumber, and that I dabbed in electricity at times.

I took him out to the garage and showed him all my new tools, most of which I had taken from work, but I didn't disclose that fact. I started up my new table saw and cut a couple pieces of wood for him. "Yes sir, you're looking at Mr. Fix It himself," I told him. A few months later it dawned on me, never tell a preacher you can build anything!

Just before they left the preacher-man said, "Seeing as how you can do all these things, surely you wouldn't mind coming out to our building site and helping on Saturday." After shooting off my big mouth I couldn't very well refuse him.

Sure enough, the next Saturday morning I was the first one on the job site. I had my new tools with me, not necessarily to use, but to show them off.

Construction on the building was in its first stages. All that was there was the basement and the block walls on the main building. That particular day they were going to put up the trusses, so one of the men put me on a wall, showed me what he wanted done, and left. They would hand me one side of a truss and I would nail it into the header on top of the wall.

After about an hour or so I noticed that no one was smoking, and I was about to have a nicotine fit. I did have enough respect for a church not to smoke in it even if it didn't have a roof. I asked one of the men to relieve me for a few minutes, and I went to my car and smoked a Winston. There was a little house on the property, and I noticed some cars would pull up to it, some ladies would take something inside, and then they would leave. I went back to my wall and stayed there until someone said to come down, as it was time to eat. We all piled into that little house. I had never seen such a spread in my life!

I sat down, grabbed a chicken leg, and took a bite out of it before I realized that I was the only one with a mouthful of food. Then, to my embarrassment, the preacher-man came in and had a word of prayer. Then it was every man for him self. I learned one thing that day, those Baptists sure could cook!

We worked until late in the evening, and as I was picking up my tools one of the men asked me if I was coming to church in the morning. I told him I had just donated my entire Saturday, and didn't he think he was being a little pushy. He said, "Come on, I want my wife to meet your wife. She needs new friends, too." I went home, headed straight for the refrigerator, and took out a six pack of Bud.

I told Margie, "Those folks want us to go to church in the morning. Maybe if you start hanging around some religious people it would do you some good." I told her that it wouldn't hurt to check it out. Besides, I wanted to see how many hypocrites from work go there. Sure enough, the next morning we put the kids on that blue and white bus, and we took our new, shiny Chevy Blazer to church. I kind of wanted to show it off anyway.

Because they didn't have their building finished, they were meeting in a rented building down town. The weather was just beginning to turn colder, and the leaves were falling from the trees. I have been told that it is the most beautiful time of the year, but, as I am color blind, I just have to take everyone's word for it.

When we arrived at the meeting place it was packed out; cars and people were everywhere. We found a seat near the back of the auditorium; better for counting hypocrites from back there. One of them came over, shook my hand, and welcomed me to the church. As he left I told Margie that he was one of the biggest jerks at work, and that I had always thought he was a holy- roller. Now I knew it for a fact.

After awhile the congregation sang a couple of songs, then the preacher-man stood up and said a few words about the new building's progress. Then came the moment I had been waiting for. Those money grabbers passed the hat to get our money. I thought to myself, a buck should cover it; after all, I had given almost my whole weekend.

The preacher-man then stood up and read something from the Bible. He talked for what seemed like forever, and he kept saying things like "getting saved," and "being born again." He finally closed his Bible, and I thought, "It's about time!" Then we all stood up and the congregation sang another song. The preacher-man was asking people to get saved. Some folks walked up to the front of the auditorium. Others met them, took their Bibles and knelt, and showed them something in their Bible. Others went up front and knelt; it looked as though they were praying or something.

By that time, I was ready to get out of there, as it was a little too much for me. At the final "Amen" I headed for the back door. I was halfway to our Blazer when I noticed that someone had cornered my wife. I got into the car and fired up a Winston. As I sat there I thought to myself, "We got that over with and the roof didn't cave in on us after all." And besides, the people all seemed friendly, and I figured it would do Margie some good.

On the following Thursday we had some visitors from the church. It was one of the men who had worked on the building, and his wife. He bragged on me and told Margie what a big help I was. Before they left he had talked me into working on the building again the following Saturday. I met some more men on that Saturday. They seemed like regular folks, not some religious nuts. Once again, before leaving, I had promised I would be in church the next day.

That Sunday we sent the kids on the bus, as usual, and we drove our freshly waxed Blazer. Again I found a back seat so I wouldn't have any trouble getting out of there at the final "Amen". The church service was about the same, the only difference being I recognized more of the people from having worked on the building. After the congregation sang a few songs they took our money again, then the preacher-man stood up to preach.

He read something from the Bible, and again he mentioned getting saved and that we were all sinners. I nudged Margie in the side and said, "He must be talking to you." The preacher mentioned that Jesus died and arose again on the third day. He mentioned Hell a few times, then said something about receiving Christ as your personal Savior. He said that Jesus was the only way to Heaven.

Things were going pretty well until that last song (invitational). I felt awkward; I thought about what the preacher had said about sinners going to Hell. As far as I was concerned they could do away with this part of church. Finally, at the final "Amen" I grabbed Margie and headed for the door. I didn't mind helping on the building and donating my Saturday, but this preaching business was making me feel uncomfortable.

On the next Thursday, just like the previous two Thursdays, we had more visitors. This time it was the ladies who had cornered Margie after church on our first visit to the church. They were Sunday school teachers, and our girls were in their classes. So, after they told us what good daughters we had, they left. I thought to myself, well at least they didn't ask me to work on their building on Saturday.

At about 6:00 o'clock that evening the preacher phoned and said they needed to use my new table saw, and that I could bring it with me on Saturday. I have to admit I enjoyed working with these new friends on the church building. It had taken the place of hang-gliding, jogging and golfing, and besides, all that good food was great! I told some of the guys at work that I had gone to church a couple of times, and most of them had some smart remarks about money, hypocrites or God (Big Daddy in the sky). One of my best friends started calling me "preacher", I told him to just keep all that money rolling in.

On Saturday I loaded up my table saw and headed to work on the church building. There weren't as many men working on the building because we were running some electrical conduit or something, but that didn't seem to hurt the size of the meal we had at lunch- time. By this time Margie was helping to provide some of the victuals at what was referred to as the "work party." Before I left for home I found myself voluntarily telling the men that I would see them in church the next morning. I couldn't believe what I was saying! I didn't want to admit that all this was new and exciting for me. It was like a breath of fresh air being with these new friends.

On Sunday we got up early to get ready for church. I kept looking for that blue and white bus, but it didn't show. By this time the kids were fighting with each other, I couldn't find a pair of socks that matched, and Margie still had her hair in curlers. I knocked on the bathroom door and started yelling at her about not being able to find a pair of socks. She came back with some wise answer. Before long everyone was screaming at each other. Then it dawned on me that we were supposed to set our clocks back one hour the night before, and that we had gotten up an hour early. I picked up my Bible and threw it across the living room. I said, "This is stupid! What am I doing up this early on a weekend anyway?" I told Margie, "You and your kids can join them holy rollers; I'm going back to bed like a normal person."

About ten minutes later I heard the horn blow on that old blue and white bus, and Margie hustled the girls out the door. After a little while I came out of the bedroom, had a cup of coffee, then asked Margie, "Do you want to go to church today?" "If you do," she replied. I said, "If we don't hurry we'll be late."

When we arrived at church we were met at the door by some of the folks who had come to our house to visit. Again we sang a few songs, they passed the hat, then the preacher stood up to preach. He read the Bible, he said that we were all sinners, and because of sin we must some day die. He said that God had a free gift for the human race, and that gift was eternal life through His son, Jesus Christ. By this time the preacher had gotten my attention. He said coming to church wouldn't get a person to Heaven. Then I thought to myself, "If that is the case, then why am I here?"

The preacher said if we want to go to Heaven we must realize that we're a sinner, we must believe that Jesus Christ died and arose again on the third day to pay that sin debt for us. He said that whoever would ask Jesus to "save" them, He would. All of this was beginning to make sense to me; after three Sundays it was finally starting to sink in. The preacher then closed his Bible, I let out a sigh of relief, and we all stood and started singing the last song. This was the part I didn't like, and why did I feel like

I was the only person he was talking to?

As they began to sing the preacher asked, "Would you like to be saved today?" I then started getting flashbacks across my mind's eye of the six pack of Budweiser in my refrigerator at home. The preacher stopped the music and said, "We have no promise of tomorrow. You could die in a car accident on your way home." A couple of people went up to the front, and once again some folks took their Bibles and knelt with them. By this time the palms of my hands were in a cold sweat and my head was throbbing. I wondered what was wrong with me. I just wanted to get out of there.

The preacher stopped the singing, once again, and told every one to bow their heads for just a moment. He then asked if there was anyone there who was not saved, that had never accepted Jesus Christ as their personal Savior, and did they want him to pray for them, if so, to raise their hands. I decided it wouldn't hurt if the preacher prayed for me, so I raised my hand up to where the preacher could see it. Then it got real quiet, and someone was tapping me on the shoulder; it was the preacher!

He had left the pulpit and walked all the way back to where I was standing. He said, "Mr. Delli, wouldn't you like to get saved this morning?" I was still having flashbacks of the six pack of beer in my refrigerator, and then the thought hit me, I would be a hypocrite if I did that. The preacher said, "It won't get any easier next Sunday." Boy, I knew that for a fact!

I then said, "Sure, why not?" and I stepped out into the aisle. We had taken a couple of steps when the preacher stopped, motioned to my wife, and said, "Won't you join your husband?" and with tears in her eyes she stepped out in the aisle also. As I reflect back on that moment I can remember being at the front of the auditorium, one of the men had taken his Bible and was showing me how to be saved, and as I looked up I saw a beautiful sight; Margie was on her knees praying. It was years later that she told me she had been praying mostly for me that I would get saved.

After I was shown from the Bible what I had heard from the pulpit for the past three Sundays, I prayed the best I knew how and asked Jesus to save my soul.

Those of you who are reading this book, if you don't know for sure that if you were to die today that you would go to Heaven, please take time to read the next few paragraphs very carefully.

* * * * * * * * * *

In order to be saved we have to realize some things. First, we must realize that we have inherited a sinful nature from Adam and Eve (Romans 5:12) thus making the entire human race sinners (Romans 3:10,23).

Then repent of that sin. (Luke 13:3)

Second, we must realize that God Almighty has a free gift for us and that gift is eternal life through His Son, Jesus Christ (Romans 6:23).

Third, we must realize that Jesus died for the sins of the world, and that He was buried and rose again on the third day. This is what the gospel is, whereby we are saved (I Corinthians 15:1-4).

Then all we have to do is to call on Him, pray to Him, and ask Him to save our soul (Romans 10:13).

Why don't you, right now, bow your head, and with childlike faith pray the following prayer, "Dear God, have mercy on me, a sinner. I believe that Jesus died for me, that He was buried, and that He rose again the third day, and by faith I am now relying on, and trusting in Jesus for the salvation of my soul. Amen."

The Bible states that you now have everlasting life (John 3:16) and that you can know you are saved now (I John 5:11,13). If you prayed the above prayer and you are relying on, or trusting in Jesus Christ, and Jesus Christ only for the salvation of your soul, then you have passed from death into life (John 5:24).

* * * * * * * * * *

Now that you are saved, you need to find a good, Bible- preaching church, one that teaches we are saved by grace and not by works (Ephesians 2:8,9). Find a church that has a soul-winning program. After you have been baptized by emersion to show the death, burial, and resurrection of Jesus Christ, then you need to join that church.

The most important thing in your early Christian life is to be faithful to all the services and read your Bible daily, starting with the book of John. Always keep your eyes on Jesus and not on people.

If you have received Jesus Christ as your personal Savior as a result of reading this book, please drop us a line so we can rejoice with you, and let us be encouraged in the Lord. Write: Larry Delli, P.O. Box 224, LaPorte, Indiana 46350.

NOT PERFECT - JUST FORGIVEN

When I had finished praying I didn't cry; some good people do. I didn't feel any great weight lifted off my shoulders; some good people do. I didn't shout; some good people do. I didn't do cartwheels down the aisle; some good people do. What I did do was to realize that I had the same headache I had before I got saved.

I stood up and joined my wife, then the preacher announced that I had just gotten saved, and that Margie had rededicated her life to the Lord. She had been saved at the age of eight years old. Some of the folks came up to us and shook our hands; some of them were crying. I didn't realize, like most new converts, what had just taken place.

When we arrived home, after the services, I went in the bedroom and changed my clothes. I took out my Bible and sat down at the kitchen table. I got a Winston out of the pack and lit one up, then I got a Budweiser out of the refrigerator. There I was, a brand new Christian, reading my Bible, drinking a beer, and smoking a cigarette. After a little while Margie came into the kitchen, looked at me, and said, "You stinking hypocrite, I thought you got saved this morning."

As usual I had to come back with a smart answer, and I said, "Maybe it didn't take."For the first time ever something felt as though a sword was piercing my heart and soul, because what she said was true. I found out later why I felt the way I did; it was the Holy Spirit of God who was piercing my heart. He had just moved into my body an hour before. My body was now a temple of the Holy Ghost (I Corinthians 6:19,20) and I was grieving Him with sin.

The next Saturday the church had a spaghetti dinner, and we had a great time. I was getting used to being around this kind of people. Two weeks later Margie and I were baptized in a church building about ten miles from the rented building we were meeting in. I had invited some of the guys from work, but none of them came.

My old friends told me that I would be alright once I got over this religious kick I was on, but I couldn't blame them for their attitude because they had seen me go from one hobby horse to another, trying to fill that void in my life. What they didn't know until years later was that void was filled in the person of Jesus Christ.

The day after I received Jesus Christ as my own personal Savior I went to work and told some of the religious guys what I had done. I found one of them in his work area, I told him that I had been to church the day before and that I had gotten religion. I didn't have all the religious jargon down yet, after all, I had only been saved for less than twenty-four hours. I suppose I was expecting him to congratulate me, but all he could find to say was "I hope you can hold out to the end." That is why I hadn't gone to church for almost twenty-nine years, because I knew that I couldn't hold out, so why bother.

As I look back on my Christian life I compare it to a weight lifter. When a person buys a set of weights they don't try to lift the full four hundred pounds the first week. No, they lift a little at a time. The more they practice with what they can handle, the stronger they become. Once they are strong

GETTING STRONGER

enough, they then add more weight, thus making them a stronger athlete. If one disregards the weights, then one will never be a strong person.

I learned that in order to be a strong Christian I first had to be able to handle the heartache and burdens of a young Christian before taking on more burdens. Just like in weight lifting, handle a little at first, then advance to heavier weights, thus making a stronger person.

Less than twenty-four hours after I was saved I was handed a weight. At first I thought it was too much for me to handle. This weight was, "Will I be able to hold out to the end?"

As I ponder those days I can see the providence of God working in my life. There were some mature Christians whom I worked with from time to time. It was these men who helped me get through this baby stage of my Christian life. One of these men was a fellow by the name of John Bennett. John was a big man who resembled an ex-boxer, one who had lost all his fights. John was always asking me to go to church with him. Every time his church had something going on he would always invite me. John was transferred to nights a couple of months before I became a Christian. I was going up a flight of stairs at work one day to the machine shop, and John was coming down. He had been put back on day shift the day before.

When John saw me he said, "Hey, Larry, we are having a guest speaker at church. Why don't you come out?"

I looked him in the eye and said, "No way man, I have my own church to go to. And not only that, I've been saved and baptized." John immediately thought I was giving him a rough time, just like always, then it dawned on him that perhaps I was serious. He acted as though he would like to believe me, but he wasn't sure if he should. He just stood there staring at me, and scratching his head as I continued going up the stairs.

It has been said that people will not always believe what you say, but they will believe what you live. The next day at lunch- time John came over to the pipe shop where I was working. I had gotten his attention the day before on the stairs, and now he wanted to know what church I was attending. When I told him, he became even more interested because, at that time, it was the fastest growing church in the area. As we talked I learned that the church where Margie and I were baptized was the church where John and his family were attending.

John kept asking me over and over again what I did, and how I did it, and how did I get in church. The poor guy became more excited each time I told him. I still didn't have the lingo down, but I explained it to him the best I knew how. From then on John took me under his spiritual wing. We started having lunch together. John opened up a whole, new, world to me. He showed me things in the Bible that I never knew existed.

A WHOLE NEW WORLD

By now the whole gang was beginning to shun me, because to them I had turned into a fanatic, and they didn't want any of it to rub off onto them.

A couple of months later John asked me if I would like to go to a Jack Van Impe crusade with him in South Bend, Indiana. I told him, "Sure, why not?" I can still remember how awkward I felt, walking down the city street with a Bible under my arm. Jack Van Impe had the entire New Testament memorized, and he preached that night on being saved; being born again. John obviously wasn't convinced yet that I was saved, because during the last song he asked me if I wanted to go down to the front and receive Jesus as my Savior. I told him I had done that already at my church, but if he thought it was the right thing to do, then, let's go. That night John knew for sure, that something had happened to this Pipefitter who was always trying to embarrass him.

John was taking a Scripture memorization course, and he gave me one of the booklets. Every time we saw each other at work we would quote Scripture to each other.

I used to work the 5:30 a.m. to 1:30 p.m. shift. When I arrived for work I was usually the only person on the ten-acre complex. It was my job to turn on the steam for the washing of parts before they could be painted. I would memorize a lot of Scripture during that time. There was a large warehouse with a little shack in it, and the main sprinkler head was in that shack, along with a couple of heat lamps to keep them from freezing. As a new Christian, I would go to this shack every morning and pray that the fellows I worked with would become Christians also. I would lie flat on my face, and as I was lying prostrate on the floor I would pray to God to give my buddies the same thing I had gotten. Praise the Lord, many of them did get what I had gotten; some right away, some years later.

Before I received Christ as my personal Savior I would play basketball on Sunday afternoons with a team from work. One of the fellows on the team was a tall, black man by the name of Al Isabell. We all called him "Big Al" because he stood six feet and six inches tall. The truth of the matter, Al wasn't that good of a basketball player, but his size would intimidate the other team, especially under the boards.

One day at work Al came over to me at break-time and told me he wouldn't be playing basketball with us anymore. I became upset and asked him why not? He replied that he was giving his Sundays to the Lord. I really blew up then, because we were relying on him. I asked, "How can playing basketball be a sin?" He didn't have an answer. I then said a lot of things that I am sure hurt him as I tried to embarrass him in front of the boys; that was my specialty.

A couple of weeks later, "Big Al" was transferred to the second shift working on the assembly line. A month or so after that I got saved. One day I was on my way to the coffee machine at break-time. There was a large group of people in line for coffee, so I positioned myself at the end of the line. As I was standing there I saw "Big Al" working on a plow mecha- nism, and it looked as though it wasn't going very well. Most of the parts had to be beaten into place. Al had a big hammer in his hand trying to make a part fit. Some of the people in the break area were laughing at him. I moseyed over to him and said, "Hi, Al." He looked up momentarily, perspiration running down his face. He just kept on pounding on that part. I said, "Al, I've got some good news."

Finally, he threw down his hammer and said, "Oh yeah? What is it?" I replied, "I got saved!"

Big Al's eyes became so big I thought they would pop out of his head. He grabbed me around the waist, literally picked me up, and started yelling, "Praise the Lord, praise the Lord!" Needless to say, it was my turn to be embarrassed. At first the folks at the break area thought there was a fight going on.

As I look back on those early days of my Christianity, I was always telling people that I was saved. Bless the Lord, it did take after all! I had boldness, and I wanted others to have what I had. I am afraid that one of the best, kept secrets at our work place, is we are a believer in Jesus Christ. No one had to ask me if I meant it when I prayed the sinner's prayer. Even though I still had a lot of bad and wicked habits that I had collected over the past twenty-nine years, I still took my stand for Jesus Christ, how about you, Christian? I know we are not perfect, but we are forgiven. Someone told you about the saving knowledge of Christ; the least you could do is pass the word along to the folks you rub elbows with every day!

I found out that "Big Al" was having a Bible study at lunch time in the old abandoned shower room. I began attending these meetings. If you want to take a stand for Christ, try carrying your Bible around with you at work. Al would open the service with a song, such as, Amazing Grace, then he would read some Scripture and teach from there.

I was having the time of my life, even though the guys in the pipe shop where I worked avoided me as though I had the plague. After all, three months earlier we had all sat at the same bar together for hours complaining about our boss and work in general. I was beginning to pick up a new vocabulary and trying to do away with the old one. There were times the guys would make me quite angry about something that didn't amount to much, then they would say to me, "I didn't think Christians were supposed to get mad." Then they would laugh at me.

A couple of months after I began attending "Big Al's" meetings he told me that he was going to quit his job in the factory and serve the Lord full time. I told him that he needed to use a little common sense and keep his good paying job. I also told him he was taking this Christianity business a little too seriously. Little did I know that less than two years from then I would be doing the same thing, with a wife and four children.

It is amazing how the Lord puts people in our path just when we need them as an encouragement, a brook in the way. I needed the guys at my work place to show me the way, to show me what real faith was all about. There may be a new, zealous, Christian in your work area with zeal, but probably doesn't have a lot of wisdom yet. Take him under your wing, be patient, and most of all, be a friend.

After attending church for a few months, I learned that no one can be saved without the aid of another human being. If someone accepts Christ as personal Savior while reading the Bible, someone had to print that Bible. If someone gets born again by listening to the radio, someone had to be broadcasting on the radio. The only way to understand salvation is through the Word of God. The only way we can have faith is by understanding the Bible. Romans 10:17 states that faith cometh by hearing, and hearing by the Word of God. I also learned that one doesn't have to be a preacher to show people how to be saved using the Bible.

This good news excited me. After all, someone loved me enough to tell me my need of salvation in Christ, the least I could do was to tell someone else.

MY FIRST SOUL

It has been estimated that approximately ninety-five percent of all church members have never led anyone to Christ. How sad! Most Christians think that is what the preacher is paid to do. I am afraid they're terribly mistaken, and they are missing many blessings because of it.

I was given some literature on what verses to use out of a book in the Bible called Romans. It was written to the church in Rome from Saint Paul. Paul was writing to these folks in Rome a letter, or epistle, to tell them how to be saved, or become genuine Christians. Isn't it strange that our modern churches of today never mention words like "being saved?" We hear a lot about being baptized, taking communion, confession to a priest, praying to Mary, praying the rosary, joining the church, confirmation, but not much anymore about being saved! Paul used the word often throughout the whole New Testament. If people want to go to Heaven they must be saved (born again,) born from above. People don't need a church, Ceremony, or ritual, people need a savior, and that Savior is Jesus Christ. I took the literature home with me and started memorizing the verses that were needed.

I will never forget the first time I told someone how to become a Christian. It was approximately one o'clock in the morning when a lady called my wife. She was having some personal problems and needed someone to talk to. At first I became upset. Why do people have to call at this ungodly hour? After a little while Margie came back to bed and told me about the conversation she had had on the phone. As I was lying there it dawned on me that the answer to this person's problems was Jesus Christ. I got up out of bed, then I called the lady back.

After conversing for about half an hour I then shared with her how Jesus Christ had turned my whole life around and gave me purpose and meaning. I asked her if she was a Christian, not just a church member, but a true Christian. She had been attending a church where they didn't mention anything about being saved. So, with my notes in front of me, I told her how to receive God's free gift of eternal life through the person of Jesus Christ. I asked her if she would like to be saved. She started crying over the phone, then said, "Yes." There we were at approximately two o'clock in the morning. Over the telephone this hungry heart prayed and asked Jesus Christ to become her personal Savior and to save her soul.

As I hung up the phone I became excited about what had just taken place. I woke my wife up and told her what had happened, but she just rolled over and went back to sleep. The lady I had witnessed to over the phone had no doubt gone to bed, but something happened that night. A spark had started a fire in my soul. Since then I have shared the good news with hundreds of hungry souls, yes, even thousands.

I felt as though I was walking on air. Could it be that a fellow could do this kind of thing for a living, I mean, as a preacher? Sure they could, but not me. I finally had a good paying job with benefits, a new car, a new home, plus the kids. As I laid my head on my pillow that night I dreamed dreams.

One of my first responsibilities as a new Christian was to keep gasoline in those blue and white buses that were going all over town. It has been said that God never puts a person in a place too small to grow in. I had to put the gasoline in on Saturday afternoon or it would be stolen by Sunday morning.

I have learned over the years to never give a person a job in the Lord's work until they have proven themselves. There was a time in my ministry when I had to replace a piano player because he kept threatening to quit every time we disagreed on something. It was a lesson I had to learn. He should have been given a job with little recognition or praise from other people. If that had been accomplished faithfully, perhaps then he would have been worthy of the title of church pianist. There are many church positions being filled with people who are seeking praise and not wanting to serve the Lord.

Once I was found faithful in refueling the buses, I was then approached about becoming a Sunday school teacher, then an usher, bus driver, and then finally a deacon.

BUMPY ROAD AHEAD

As I mentioned earlier, the day I became a Christian I had a case of Budweiser in my refrigerator. I felt there was no use in throwing it out, so I drank it. It was such a natural thing to buy a case of beer every week, so the next week when Margie went grocery shopping I had her pick up another one. It lasted for about three weeks, then I told her I was going to start cutting back, and if I wanted any more I would buy it myself (this pleased her immensely because she never liked buying beer anyway). I didn't want to sound too fanatical about my drinking even though it had almost destroyed our home. That has been fifteen years ago and I haven't had any since. I am afraid some of you readers have been saved for years and are still sucking on the bottle. You didn't get what I got that day in that little rented building years ago. Booze had made life miserable for me, my family, and for those who were close to us. The Lord took that awful desire for drink away from me almost immediately, and I praise Him for that!

My smoking habit was a little different story. Don't get me wrong, smoking and drinking doesn't send people to Hell. Only the rejection of Jesus Christ as Savior does that, but these habits are a bad testimony for a Christian. You may be reading this and saying to yourself, "I know preachers who smoke," and that may be true. I know for a fact that in some churches the folks have a smoke break between Sunday school and church services. For the average person to see a group of men standing out in front of a bar smoking, it looks natural, but for the same person to see a group of men standing outside of church smoking, he calls them hypocrites and phonies. People outside of church want to see something different in us Christians!

Before I became a Christian this fellow at work who smoked big, nasty smelling cigars would tell me, as he blew smoke in my face, that if I didn't get saved I was going to split Hell wide open. I would think to myself, "If this cigar-smoking freight train is going to Heaven, I have nothing to worry about."

I became so under conviction about my smoking I wouldn't smoke in public anymore. I didn't want my two daughters, Lori and Marla, to know that little white stick could control me. I would go into my own bathroom, open the window, put a towel on the floor against the crack at the bottom of the door, then light up a cigarette and blow the smoke out the window. No, smoking won't send you to Hell, but it makes your teeth yellow, and it doesn't do your lungs any good either. Not all things come easy for a new Christian. If you have been a Christian for awhile, and know someone who is struggling with the smoke habit, or the drinking habit, don't shun them. Help them if you can, and be their friend.

Overall, things were going pretty well. Our marriage was doing better, we had made some new friends, and our old friends didn't come around much any more. Margie was expecting our third daughter, Melissa Lynn, who was born a month or so later. I was just beginning to learn some Bible principles that I could apply to my own life. I saw the need to set the example for my children, of going to church and helping any way I could. I was getting a grip on the Bible principle of finances, and trying to get my life under control in that area. I learned early that the more I gave, the more I got. I was taught to tithe my income by giving God ten percent. At first I didn't know how I was going to afford to do that. Before I became a Christian our house payment was one hundred and fifteen dollars per month, and I was always broke. Just before I received Jesus into my life we bought a new house, and our payments were double what we had been paying on our first house. I started tithing by faith, and I always had a few bucks left over. It didn't make any sense, but it does work, I promise.

About six months after my salvation experience it seemed as though the bottom had fallen out of the whole thing. I was attending church on Wednesday nights. Some of you readers have been saved for years and still don't attend Wednesday nights regularly. Shame on you! If you only knew what an encouragement you could be to your pastor, you would be more faithful to the services. On one Wednesday night service one of the men called me over to the side and said, "Did you hear the news?"
"No," I answered.

He said, "One of the deacons was arrested for indecent exposure on a public school playground." The deacon had worked with me on the church building for months. He was an older man and a sharp dresser. You know the type, every hair had to be in place, his clothing had to match, and when he spoke there wasn't any dangling participles. He had red hair and had a large, brown mole on his neck, which he often hid by wearing a turtleneck sweater.

I couldn't believe what I was hearing. This fellow was a new hero of mine. He sang in the church choir, he taught a Sunday school class, he drove a church bus, and attended every service. At first I became angry at the Devil for spreading this awful lie. This deacon stood that night at church and said the newspaper had made a mistake, that it was untrue. To my disappointment, the next day, under oath, he pleaded guilty to all charges.

Our church at that time was running about four hundred in attendance, but by the time this scandal blew over we were struggling to reach one hundred in Sunday school. This deacon, of course, was relieved of all his responsibilities in the church and was not allowed to have any leadership role. Rumors were running around like wildfire. People would call me up and ask all kinds of questions. Church members were leaving the church like rats leaving a sinking ship, mostly those I looked up to as spiritual leaders. For reasons unknown to me the fellow would not leave the church. He continued to stay and make waves for the church leadership.

After the service on Sunday morning the pastor dismissed all the visitors. He read from Matthew 18:15-18 about church discipline. A police officer, who was a member of the church, stood and read all the charges against the deacon from official police documents. There was a court order prohibiting him from entering church property. This was a difficult time for all involved, and some have never recovered from this incident.

As I muse these days of my early Christian life, I can see God's providence at work in my life. What appeared to be mature Christians were quitting the church and God. Because I was still a relatively young Christian, I had my eyes on the Lord and not on man. Sure, I was hurt and disappointed in what had happened, but life must go on. I felt as though a weight had been placed on my shoulders, and just like a weight lifter, I had to struggle with it until I became a strong enough Christian to handle it.

In recent months some of our TV preachers have been found out, and thousands of people are quitting God and the church because of the scandals. The trouble is most of them had their eyes on man and not on God. Man is weak with a sinful nature, and different men have different temptations. Man will let you down, but God never will. We must keep our eyes on the Lord. If this incident had occurred later on in my Christian life, perhaps I would have joined the others, God only knows.

During these difficult days the pastor hired an associate pastor to help lighten the load, but unfortunately the new, young, zealous associate seemed to think he could handle the situation and the church better than the pastor-founder. I was quite naive in those early days and was taken in by this wolf in sheep's clothing. He was a tall, slim fellow with a southern accent, and he had a premature white streak on the left, front side of his hair. This

GETTING STRONGER

associate would call me on the phone and ask questions about the pastor, such as, "When was the last time the pastor brought anyone to church?" or "Did you ever notice how the preacher's kids are always late for church?"

I didn't see then what he was doing, but he was undermining the pastor's authority, and putting doubt in my mind about his competency. I wasn't the only one whom he called to talk about some of the things that were going on in the church. I was learning in my young Christian life that, not everything that glitters is gold. Approximately a year after the associate pastor was hired the church was divided between him and the pastor. The pastor was finally forced to let the associate pastor go, and when he left, so did some more of the people. By this time the church was struggling just to make ends meet. It was another weight I had to struggle with, and just like a weight lifter I labored with it until I could handle it. I could have cast the weight aside and quit the church and God, but I chose to struggle with it so that I would become a better Christian. As I look back on those days, I believe it was a miracle that I still wanted to serve the Lord.

FULL SURRENDER

I was transferred to the second shift at work in the maintenance department. I decided I would start a Bible study, just like Big Al had done on the day shift. We met in the pipe shop, which was in the main power-house. The power-house produced all the electricity and steam for the entire plant. When at first I began these Bible studies just me, and one other fellow; who was a new Christian and was eager to learn, were in attendance. For the most part I taught what I knew best, how to become a true Christian. I had a blackboard I used to draw pictures on dealing with salvation. I gave away plaques with Scripture verses on them to anyone who brought a visitor. We had as many as eighteen men and women who gathered together to hear the Word of God. I loved it, but just like anything else one tries to do for the Lord, I received my share of criticism. As a result of the Bible studies many of the folks who came to classes received Jesus Christ as their personal Savior.

I was called one night to an area to do some maintenance work, but because the plant was so large each one of the maintenance men had their own three- wheel bicycle to get from one job to another. On my bicycle there was a wire basket on the back. This is where I carried all my tools. I was called to the weld floor to repair an air- line, I parked my bicycle and looked the job over. When I returned to my bicycle all my tools were gone and, as I recall, there were at least two hundred dollars worth. At first I thought someone was playing a trick on me, but as time passed I realized that I had been ripped off.

One day, a couple of weeks later, as I was riding my bicycle through the weld floor area, a big fellow, a weldor, yelled at me to stop; when someone that big yells at me I either speed up or stop. I stopped and he asked, "Is you the preacher?" "I'm a Christian," I replied. He bowed his head and said, "I stole your tools." I didn't know what to say. He then opened a large tool chest and brought out my tool- box.

He said, "I stole them two weeks ago and I haven't had a good night's sleep since then. I'm sorry." He put the tools in the basket on my bicycle, and as he did so I told him I appreciated his restoring them. I asked him if he was a Christian, and he said he used to go to church all the time, but hadn't been in years. I shook his gigantic hand and said, "It sounds as though the Lord is trying to tell you something," and then I rode off.

We had a large variety of people coming to the Bible study. Some believed just the way I did, and some didn't. I can remember being asked questions about things I had never heard of up until then, but it was the experience that made me study my Bible even more. We had a little gal coming to the Bible study who was a welder. I imagine God was proud of her as she carried her welding helmet in one hand and her King James Version of the Bible in the other. There was no room for doubt about where she stood for the Lord.

About a month before Barb started coming to the Bible studies I had told a fellow by the name of Ed how to be saved and become a Christian. Ed accepted the Lord as his Savior and started attending the Bible studies. One day, as I was teaching, I noticed my welder friend, Barb, and my fork lift driver friend, Ed, looking at each other with a twinkle in their eyes. It was love at first sight. It was close to a year later that they were married, attending church together, and serving the Lord happily.

I like those types of stories, with a happy ending, but not all of them turn out that way. After Barb and Ed got involved in the Bible studies, I met another couple. I had gone to visit an old high school buddy of mine, but he had moved; however, his older brother had moved in, and he invited me in. He had gotten remarried. His new wife had six children from her previous marriage, so there were kids all over the place. He and his new wife sat with me at the kitchen table. After fifteen minutes or so, I shared with them how the Lord had come into my life. I shared Jesus Christ with them, and about an hour later with tears in their eyes they bowed their heads together and asked Jesus Christ to save their souls. It was beautiful. I visited them a couple of weeks later and they were attending church together, all fifteen of them.

After a month or so, we moved out of the area. It wasn't until two years later that I went to visit them. They weren't home, so I went across the street to his mother's house. She invited me in and told me that her son, Dick, and his wife, Mary, had gotten a divorce some six months earlier. She also said that only a week and one- half earlier Mary had come running out of a bar and was hit by a passing car. Mary died instantly. Dick had quit his job and all he did was to hang out at the local pool hall up town. I couldn't believe it! What had happened? The last time I had seen them they were the happiest people in the world.

As I reminisce about these two couples, I believe I can see why one ended happily and the other ended in disaster. When Barb and Ed met Jesus Christ, He became the center of their lives. They prayed together, went to church together, and studied their Bibles together. The old saying, "Those who pray together, stay together," is true. On the other hand, Dick and Mary started missing church, and never really grew in the Lord. After awhile their priority switched from Jesus Christ back to the things of the world. When the pressures of life closed in on them, they started thinking of themselves instead of each other. Sad, but true, most marital problems arise because of one's pride. It drove them apart, kept them from the only one who could help, which was the Lord Jesus. The saddest thing of all is the thirteen children who, for a short time, saw their parents at their happiest, and then watched them drop to the bottom.

Being in maintenance I had the run of the entire plant. That enabled me to witness for the Lord. I would put gospel tracts in the restrooms, both men's and women's. When one takes a stand for the Lord it doesn't take long to find out who their friends are and who isn't. I made up my mind early in my Christian experience that, "As for me and my house, we will serve the Lord."

STEP OF FAITH

One day I came across John Bennett, the fellow who looked like a boxer who had lost all his fights. John had decided to go to Bible College some fifty miles away. He was going to drive back and forth each day, that way he could keep his good paying job. He was excited about going and asked me if I would like to go with him. He was going to take just a couple of classes, nothing serious. It seemed exciting to me, and we would split the cost of gasoline. After much prayer and fasting I decided I would at least give it a shot.

By the time I decided to go to Bible College, John had talked himself out of going. John was afraid of failure. Most everyone has what is called a "comfort Zone" where we feel at ease, no extra pressure or obligation. After thinking it over John thought going to Bible College would be far beyond his comfort zone. What John did not know was he had gotten me excited about going, and I had been praying about attending for weeks and had perfect peace. I will never forget the reaction of my wife as I said, "Honey, what would you think if I went to Bible College?"

To my surprise she said, "I'll divorce you." Then she said, "What on earth are you thinking of? We finally after ten years of struggling, have some things that we don't have to be ashamed of. You have a good job, three beautiful daughters, a new house, a decent car, and now this!" After a couple of days praying about it she told me that whatever I thought was best she would back me up one hundred percent.

After the first ten miserable years of our marriage I really couldn't blame her, and besides, it wasn't as if I was going to give up my job or anything. I decided to commute back and forth. I wasn't sure if I could hack the drive, studies and work all at once. I sent away for an application form. When I received it in the mail a few days later, I took it into my bedroom. I was excited as I took out a Winston, lit it up, and began filling out the application. On the application there was a question wanting to know if I used alcohol in any form. I marked "no," as I hadn't had a beer in almost a year. There was also the question wanting to know if I attended Hollywood movies, I answered this question in the negative also. When I came to the question wanting to know if I used tobacco in any form, I skipped it and went on to the next one.

When I had finished filling out the application I went back to the tobacco question. I picked up that Winston, took one long drag from it, then I butted it. I then put "no" on the application form for my answer about tobacco. That has been almost sixteen years ago, and I haven't had a cigarette since, praise the Lord! It was as though God was saying to me, "Is this for real or are you just playing church?" Believe me, it's real!

Hyles-Anderson College was about fifty miles away, one way, and with me working the second shift I could just make it home in time to start work on time. My very first day at school I punched in late for work. My boss, who used to be an old drinking buddy of mine, read me the riot act. He acted as though he thought I was a complete idiot. He said a man thirty years old should know better than to start something he will never finish. It was strange how the old gang turned on me. The more I tried to do for the Lord, the worse they became.

So there I was, driving over one hundred miles a day, working from between forty and forty-eight hours a week, teaching a Bible class at work, driving a Sunday school bus and teaching a Sunday school class. One thing I did learn during this time, and that was discipline. Discipline to the clock; I didn't have a lot of free time to waste, or unfortunately, to be with my family either. After being out of school for so long I had to learn all over again how to study. My first English class was actually the other students' second semester for the class, seeing as how I started school in January. I didn't get the basics in high school so it was all the more difficult. I didn't know an adverb from a verb. I was thirty years old and I realized this would probably be my last chance at something like this, so I gave it my best. I did manage to finish with a "B" average overall.

After about a year and one half of commuting to college, I was told one day after chapel that I had a message at the information desk. Sure enough, just as I had suspected, Margie had just left for the hospital to deliver our fourth child. I cut my last class and headed for home. I took my time. I had missed my first daughter's, Lori Marie, birth because I was over-seas. I missed my second daughter's, Marla Ann, birth because she was born in Lake City, Florida, and I was working in St. Augustine, Florida, some ninety miles away. I did show up for our third daughter's, Melissa Lynn, birth, so what was the big deal? I couldn't do anything but wait anyway. I stopped and bought myself a milk shake.

When I arrived at the hospital I went to the labor room, but Margie wasn't there, so I moseyed on down to the delivery room and poked my head in the door. "Hi honey, I'm here," I said.

Just then this little nurse, who looked like a Marine Drill Sergeant, said to me, "It's about time you got here." She barked, "Here, put on this cap and gown, take off your shoes and put on these slippers."

I said, "Wait a minute lady, you don't understand, I've got a weak stomach. I get sick when I cut open a watermelon and it's too ripe."

She replied, "Never mind buster. This will probably be your last one, and you need to see it happen."

I sure didn't expect this or I wouldn't have cut my last class. Before I knew what was happening, there I was, sitting at the head of the delivery table. There was a big mirror at the other end so I could see the whole thing. About that time the doctor came in, scrubbed up, put on rubber gloves, and said as he reached down to catch the baby as it came out, "Why didn't someone tell me this gal was pregnant?" It all happened so quickly, but I got to see my son, Adam Christian, being born. When the doctor held him up by his feet, to show his gratitude, the little fellow urinated on his mother and the doctor. I left soon after and found an empty room, closed the door, and started weeping uncontrollably for five minutes or so. I promised God I would rear this man-child the best I could for the glory of God.

I now had a total of four children, so this would be a most opportune time to throw in the towel as far as Bible College was concerned. By now I was convinced that this was what God would have me to do at this time of my life. The drive back and forth was starting to drain me physically, and my job seemed less and less important.

One night, after I had left work, I went out to my second hand car, a sixty-six, Chevy, in the parking lot. Someone had thrown a brick through the back window. Because it was midnight, I just drove it home the way it was and went to bed. The next morning I left for school at six forty-five. Things were going pretty well until I reached the big city. A city policeman pulled me over, got out of his squad car and walked over to me. He asked for my driver's license and car registration. "Don't you know it's dangerous driving a car like this?" he said.

I thought that was a strange question, so I asked him, "What do you do about people who drive convertibles?"

"Oh, a wise guy," he said. After he gave my car a quick general inspec tion, he jumped into his police car, turned on his lights and siren, and he pealed out and went through a red light. I could see him far ahead of me as I followed him through two more lights, and then he turned off his lights and siren. I followed him another half mile or so, then he pulled into a McDonalds. I was curious about what was happening at McDonalds, so I pulled in to investigate. When I walked in the policeman was ordering breakfast. It then dawned on this country boy what he had really pulled me over for. He had wanted someone to pay for his breakfast. Just like any other profession, the police department has bad apples as well as good ones.

After two years of driving one hundred and eight miles a day, plus working full time, we decided to move nearer to the college. I will never forget the reaction of the old gang at work when I told them I was going to quit my job. They told me similarly what I had told "Big Al" a couple years earlier; "You need to use a little common sense. You have top seniority as a Pipefitter, you're thirty years old, and now you have all them kids to feed." What they didn't realize was I was almost seven thousand dollars in debt to the credit union because of my lifestyle before I became a Christian.

By this time I was into this project hook, line, and sinker. I figured if God was in it, He would have to bail me out. There were men standing in line to take over my job when I quit. What they didn't know then was that the entire factory would close down in about three years. All I did was to get a three- year head start on the rest of them. I often look back on this time of my life and think how miserable I would have been if I had quit school to keep a job that folded up anyway.

Before I quit my job I did have enough sense to get another one first. I hired into Pullman Standard, making diner train cars for Amtrak. I quit my job on Wednesday and started my new job on Thursday. I moved into the city, and stayed in a roach- infested motel until we could sell our house. I was on the job for about two weeks and, due to a misunderstanding, was fired. So there I was with no job, four kids, new house, new car, seven thousand dollars in debt, and a very disappointed wife. It was another one of those weights being placed on my shoulders, and just like a weight lifter, I would have to labor with the added weight until I became strong enough of a Christian to handle it.

After a couple of weeks of looking for work, I was financially withdrawn from school. Now I had no school, and no job. This was a time of testing my faith. Approximately a month later, I hired into a place where I was earning less than half of what I was accustomed. I was employed at a place where we made casket hardware; talk about a dead end job, this was it. I even tried to get my old job back at Allis-Chalmers, as a Pipefitter, where two months earlier I had seven years seniority, but they laughed me to scorn.

I was saying to myself, how do I get into these spots? Only this time I knew I had One with me who "sticketh closer that a brother." My faith started to stagger just a little I have to admit. We started receiving the kind of mail like we used to, you know the kind of hate-mail I'm talking about. Notification stating that they are going to take your car away, turn off your heat and water, or are coming to take their furniture back, or maybe even threaten to turn you over to a collection agency. It had been awhile since I was in this position, and I had almost forgotten how awful it felt.

Sam Smiles once said, "It is a mistake to suppose that men succeed through success. They more often succeed through failure." I hope Sam knew what he was talking about! It seems funny to me the way people shy away from you when you need them the most. I became real close to Jesus during this time. So often, when our bills are all being paid and we have a steady income, it is easy to put the only One who really cares for us on the back burner.

I was reminded of something during this time that was written on the wall of a concentration camp in Germany during WWII:
> I believe in the sun, even when it is not shining.
> I believe in love, even when it is not felt.
> I believe in God, even when He is silent.

GETTING STRONGER

During this time we sold most of our toys to pay the bills. I sold my golf clubs, all our bicycles, one car, and we were always having garage sales. We did these things to keep from having everything we owned taken away by our creditors. We finally sold our beautiful Cape Cod home, with it's four bedrooms and big back yard, and moved into some apartments nearer the college.

After six months I landed another good paying job, and I was back in college again. It is amazing how one's outlook on life is changed when one can look to the future with hope and expectation.

We moved into the big city, into an apartment complex in the poor part of town next to some railroad tracks. There were four sets of tracks less than a hundred yards from our apartment. It has been said that on an average there was a train on the tracks every seven minutes. The day we moved into the apartment was the day I realized that a three- bedroom apartment wasn't going to hold all the furniture from a four- bedroom house. We kept everything that had any value and put the rest out near the trash pick up.

As I stood gazing out the window I saw people gathering around our old furniture like a bunch of Indians surrounding a wagon train. I called my wife and children over and told them to look at those poor people fighting over our junk. Within a year I was out there with them. Every time someone moved in we would surround the garbage heap. I would kill for a lamp that worked, or a table with all four legs. It seemed as though the Lord was testing to see what we were made of, like forming a good knife: first heat is applied, then it is beat into shape, then more heat is applied, and then more forming and shaping. The more heat, the better the quality. This was a time of applying the heat, of forming and shaping us for things down the road. It has been said, "If you can't take the heat, get out of the kitchen."

The college we attended was an arm of the church we attended also. The First Baptist Church of Hammond, Indiana, would have, on the average, fifteen thousand folks in church every Sunday. Dr. Jack Hyles is the pastor, and the church has been proclaimed as the World's Largest Sunday- School. The college at that time had over two thousand students, plus a high school and elementary school. It is the only place I have ever been to where spectators took their Bibles to a football game, and the crowd would get to their feet and cheer the preacher when he arrived. It is a place where parents can start their children in kindergarten and watch as they go all the way through for a master's degree in college without leaving the Baptist influence.

My last two years at Hyles-Anderson went by fast for me, as I was so busy planning and dreaming for the future. It was similar to my junior year in high school all over again, with the future ahead.

WESTWARD HO

During my senior year in college I began seeking a place to serve the Lord. I visited my previous pastor and he told me of a place that needed a soul-winning Baptist church, but it was in the state of Washington. I sent out resumes all over America. The day finally came when I finished my studies. It had taken me four years, even though I had been financially withdrawn for six months. I had gone to three summer schools in a row, and that gave me twenty-seven extra credits. I finished up in January, but the commencement exercises weren't until May. I didn't have a place to go, but I didn't want to stay in Hammond, because I had seen too many graduates get out of college, and never go out into the work. They would have good jobs, and would stay under the security of Dr. Jack Hyles and the great First Baptist Church.

I have heard that the happiest people in the world are those who have become true Christians, and have surrendered their lives to the Lord's work. Those who have gone into the Lord's service on a full-time basis, whether paid or not, have the joy and inner peace that only a surrendered life can bring.

It has been said that the second happiest people in the world are those who are not saved. Those who are going through life carefree without any thought of tomorrow or eternity. Those people who believe weekends are made for Michelob, those folks who are engulfed in themselves and the things they have gathered along life's road. Sad, but true, their happiness will end along with their last breath.

Again, it has been said that the most miserable people in the world are those who have been saved and called into the ministry, but refuse to go, those people who would not give up the security of a good job, or a fine home, or a new car. Usually those folks are the most critical people in our churches. They're the ones who are always informing the pastor of his shortcomings, or worse yet, informing the rest of the congregation of the pastor's shortcomings. These poor, frustrated individuals usually pacify their consciences by teaching a Sunday school class or having some kind of fail-proof Bible study in their homes. Others ease their consciences by taking some kind of correspondence course and letting everyone know how spiritual they are. Sad, but true, not everyone in our churches, are an encouragement and a comfort.

I didn't go through four years of poverty to stay in Hammond, so after much prayer we decided to purchase a school bus and use it for a U-haul, then head west. By this time it was March. We bought a sixty-six, passenger bus and took all the seats out of it, except the first four. We took it down to my folks' house where I built a trailer hitch for towing our Chevy Blazer.

By this time we had gotten rid of most of our furniture and all our toys, so the bus held everything we had, which wasn't much considering almost sixteen years of marriage and four children. Dr. Jack Hyles once said, "There are two ways of being rich, being able to afford what you want or wanting only what you can afford." My folks couldn't understand why I was moving all the way out to Washington. What could I tell them? I didn't know why the doors seemed to be opening in that direction and nowhere else.

The bus we had bought was a yellow school bus that had been used by a

Christian school. I painted the windows yellow on the inside, I didn't want people looking at our junk as we traveled. I checked everything over pretty well before we left on our twenty-six hundred, mile trip.

The day finally arrived for our departure. The bus was loaded down with everything we owned. Our Chevy Blazer was hooked up to the back of the bus, and it had all our clothes in it. I disconnected the drive train on it, preventing the speedometer from registering all the miles. It was a cold, March day, about twenty degrees above zero. We had spent the night before at my mother-in-law's house. She lives across town from my parents. At five-thirty that morning I loaded up my wife and four children to travel across America to a place I had never even heard of before, let alone ever been. When we left my mother-in-law's place, we must have looked like the "Beverly Hillbillies" as we pulled out of town that morning. We were on our way to turn the state of Washington upside down for the Lord Jesus. It was a beautiful day, the sun was shining, and there was a light snowfall at the same time. We were all excited about our big adventure out west!

About twenty miles down the road I heard an awful sound coming from under the hood of the bus. I pulled over to investigate. The alternator, which weighed about fifty pounds, had broken off the wheel well, and had fallen into the fan, and the fan had cut into the radiator. That wasn't what we had planned; after all, we had another two- thousand, six- hundred, and twenty-one miles left to go.

Along about that time a state policeman pulled up behind us with his squad car lights flashing. He got out of the car, looked that old bus over, and then he said, "Where do you think you are going with this rig?"

"To Bellingham, Washington," I replied.

Then he asked, "How long have you been on the road?" When I told him twenty-five minutes he laughed right out loud, then he said, "If this thing isn't off the highway in one hour I am going to give you a ticket." I walked to the nearest farmhouse and had a farmer tow me off the highway, and into his barnyard.

It was still early in the morning, so I disconnected the Blazer, crawled under it, and hooked up the drive train. We drove to the nearest town, which was about for miles away, and went to a café where we had breakfast. The waitress informed me the local garage had an ace mechanic, so when we finished eating our breakfast, I went to see him, and he took us to his house, out of the weather, while he fixed the bus. After approximately four- hours, and a lot of running around, the bus was fixed and ready for the road.

The family all piled in the bus as I crawled under the Blazer to disconnect the drive train, then we were finally off to win the lost to Christ in Washington. I started the bus, put it in gear, but nothing happened. I got out of the bus and investigated the situation. I discovered the rear end was totally destroyed due to the lack of oil. What a disappointment! We had been on the road for half a day and gone only about twenty miles, and now the rear end of the bus was shot! It was as though a weight had been placed on my shoulders again, and this weight was extra heavy. I didn't know if I could handle it. Just like a weight lifter after he has practiced lifting a certain amount, then more weight is added, he must labor with it to become stronger, so I battled with this weight. It has been said that one can tell how much character a person has by what it takes to stop him.

I unhooked the Blazer, crawled under it, and once again hooked up the drive train enabling me to drive it. I was too proud and embarrassed to go back to my hometown and let folks know we had failed already. I had gone to high school with a fellow, who owned a junk- yard, so I went to him to buy another rear end for the bus. To save myself twenty dollars I took it out of an old truck myself.

It was already a cold day, but it seemed even more so, while I was under that old truck. By then the snow had turned into a tempest. Two hours, and

GETTING STRONGER

two hundred and fifty dollars later, I had another rear end for the bus. By this time it was getting dark outside, so I took Margie and the kids back to my mother-in-law's house, who I knew would understand if anyone could. It was close to nine o'clock that night when I crawled under that old yellow bus in that farmer's barnyard. It was snowing and blowing. When I looked the situation over I realized I didn't have a gasket, so I dabbed some permatex on the two parts and put it together. At approximately eleven o'clock I slipped back into town and parked the bus behind the church near my mother-in-law's house, then I crawled under that Blazer and unhooked the drive train for the fourth time that day. What a long day we had, and the only thing we had accomplished was to waste about eighteen hours.

TRY, TRY AGAIN

The next morning, same time as before, we loaded up and headed out. I have heard it said, "The one thing worse than a quitter is the man who is afraid to begin." It was a new day, the sun was shining, and the temperature was in the low forties. Everything seemed to be a whole lot brighter. As we drove past the spot where we had broken down the day before, we all gave a loud cheer. We were making progress! I couldn't see the Blazer from the driver's seat in the bus, so I taped a flag on a stick to the mirror on the Blazer. When I saw the flag, I knew I still had a Blazer.

Eighteen hours later, we had just gone through Des Moines, Iowa, when I heard what sounded like a siren behind us. I looked into the rearview mirror, but didn't see anything. The sound became so loud that I pulled off the freeway and into a gas station. I jumped out, started looking around, and to my dismay I learned that I had blown the permatex out of the rear end of the bus. It was so hot the gears became welded together. There we were, four hundred miles from home with a broken-down bus. It was yet another weight placed on me. If only I could wrestle with it long enough to where I could handle it, then I would become a stronger Christian because of it.

I knew only one person in the entire state of Iowa. He was a former basketball star from high school. Buzz was one of the few who had made it big playing sports. He had attended Drake University on a basketball scholarship, and when he graduated he went into real estate. I called him on the phone. He was surprised to hear from me, and was even more surprised to hear that I was now a preacher. He drove out and picked us up. As he was still a bachelor, he had plenty of room. We stayed with him for three days, during which time we were able to get another rear end for the bus in Des Moines. It cost close to two hundred dollars this time, and I spent an extra fifty cents for a gasket. After five days on the road we had only traveled four hundred miles from home and were five hundred dollars in the hole, and two thousand, two hundred and twenty-one miles away from our destination. At this rate we wouldn't reach Washington until about June and would be ten thousand dollars in debt!

Early on the fourth day after we had arrived in Des Moines, we headed out once again. Before we had left Indiana our pastor had given us a phone number to call when we went through Council Bluffs, Iowa. After ten hours on the road we stopped at a truck stop, and I called this preacher friend of our pastor. I told him who we were and where we were going. He invited us to come to his church, but I wanted to keep on going west. He insisted that he meet us, so he drove out to the truck stop. When he arrived he got out of his van and walked around that old yellow bus shaking his head. He then asked a funny question, "Where is your spare tire?" In all my planning I had forgotten about even thinking of a spare tire.

"I reckon the Lord is going to have to keep air in the ones we have," I replied.

He started shaking his head again as he walked around the bus. He said, "Either you have a lot of faith, or you're not too smart." I knew which one it was, but I didn't want him to find out. When I think about it, there is a fine line between faith and stupidity. "Our church wants to give you a little something to help you along the way," he said, and then he took out a check book and wrote us out a check for two hundred dollars. I couldn't believe it. I had never seen this preacher before in my life, but he was a brother in

Christ who wanted to fill a need. God allows the right people to cross our paths just to give us that extra boost we sometimes need. If I remember correctly, he was still shaking his head as we pulled out onto the freeway.

The next three days were uneventful, except for the dust storm we went through in Nebraska. The wind was so great that it broke off the flag that was attached to the Blazer, and since the flag was no longer there I couldn't tell if we had a car or not. The only time I knew for sure was when we pulled into a gas station. The gas gauge didn't work on the bus, so we stopped every one hundred miles and filled up. After traveling for about eight days we started to get into the mountains, which made Margie a nervous wreck, as she is terrified of heights. The kids were having the time of their lives. Behind the front four seats we had a stack of mattresses. The kids would play on them as we traveled, or take a nap.

As we were traveling along one day we saw a sign with a flashing yellow light. The sign read "chain-up area." "I wonder what that means," I said, and Margie replied, "Oh, probably nothing important." Half an hour later as we started up a mountain we realized too late what the sign had meant. When we had reached the chain-up area we were supposed to pull over and put chains on our tires, but by the time we realized this we were at the summit of the mountain in a blizzard. It was hard to believe. Only half an hour earlier it was a cold, but calm day. All of a sudden the bus began bouncing up and down at the rear end. I pulled over the best I could, keeping my foot on the brakes, and told Margie to get out and check for a flat tire. She got out into the blizzard and started kicking the tires. As we sat there on the side of a cliff, semi trucks were passing us at about ten miles an hour. As they went past us the drivers would shake their heads, and some would even shake their fists because we were creating a dangerous situation by being in a stopped position partly on the road.

Poor Margie was terrified. I know I wasn't her favorite person at that time, but what could we do? We couldn't turn around; we had no other alternative but to continue. When she got back into the bus she said, "What are you trying to do, kill me?" Then she informed me that it didn't look to her as if we had a flat tire. It didn't matter whether we did or not, we didn't have a spare tire anyway. As we started to pull back onto the road, the bus and Blazer started sliding backwards. I was getting a little nervous myself about this time. Finally the tires grabbed hold, and we had a little traction again.

The mountains became higher and higher, and steeper and steeper. If there was ever a time when I was extra close to the Lord it was on this adventure across America. The next day we were climbing, what I think was Elk Part Pass in Montana. We knew we were in for another elevated drive, because the sign said, "Incline next eight miles." I had to admit that it was beautiful. I had never seen anything like it in my life. We could see for miles. The evergreens were blowing in the breeze, and the sun coming through the windows felt extra warm.

We finally made it to the summit, and now we started our descent down the other side. This was the part that made us all nervous. We had no idea the condition of the brakes. I told the family as we were descending down the mountain, that we would stop at the next town for gas and get out and relax for a couple hours. Everyone was for that idea. We had been on the road for a week and a half, and we were all under a strain.

I think the name of the town where we decided to gas-up and take a break was Crackerville. If not, it should have been. It was close to eight o'clock in the morning, and the sky was blue with gigantic white clouds. No wonder Montana is called "Big sky country." We pulled into the only gas station in town. It was also the general store and post office, but the place was closed tight as a drum.

We began looking for a place to turn around. I took the first street to the right that I came to, thinking to go around the block, and back to the high way. The street kept going for some distance, and there were no exits. After while it turned into a gravel road. I started complaining to the Lord

113

again. I said, "Lore, you know why we are going west, to start a church that will win souls and glorify you." I then said, "Lord, this isn't fair! Here we are trying to serve you, and we're lost in some one-horse town." I asked myself, "Why do things like this have to happen?"

A mile later the gravel road turned into a dirt road. I couldn't believe what was happening; before we knew it, we were in the middle of a cow pasture. I began complaining to God once again, "This doesn't make any sense, we are wasting time." I looked into my rearview mirror and saw a strange sight. For the first time on our trip I could see our Blazer behind us. This was beginning to become one of those weights that I wasn't ready for, an extra burden. Just like a weight lifter I was going to have to toil with it until I became a strong enough Christian to handle it.

Finally I saw a farm- house in the distance on the left-hand side. As we continued, there was a little creek between us, and the farm- house. We crossed over a tiny bridge into the barnyard where we could turn around. As we made the turn our Blazer broke loose, and as I continued the turn I noticed what had happened. I stopped the bus, jumped out to inspect the situation, and found that the trailer hitch had broken in two. It then dawned on me what had just transpired; if that Blazer had broken off just twenty minutes earlier coming down that mountain, we wouldn't have known about it until we pulled in for gas. It could have rolled down that mountain like a cannon ball into oncoming traffic, killing dozens of people, or it could have run into our bus. In any case, it could have been a real disaster.

I said, "Praise the Lord!" All this time He was watching over us, and all I was doing was griping and complaining. About this time the rancher **came** out of his house. He was a tall man and looked like the outdoors type with his deep suntan. He was smoking a big cigar. He resembled what I thought a real cowboy would look like with his pistol strapped to his side. I can imagine, we looked a sight to him. He probably didn't get much company, let alone a visit from the "Beverly Hillbillies."

He looked the situation over and asked, "Can you weld? "I said, "Yes sir."

114

GETTING STRONGER

He then said, "In that shed over yonder is a welder, a grinder, and all the metal you'll need to fix your hitch." He explained that he had some cattle in the street or he would do it for me. As he left to round up his cattle, I asked myself, "What 'street'?"

The Lord had been leading this complaining preacher to the very spot where I could get help. He was saying, "If you will just stop griping and grumbling, I have a blessing for you down the road." I began to rejoice when I saw the big picture. With tears in my eyes I asked the Lord for forgiveness and thanked Him once again.

Isn't that the way life is most of the time, griping and complaining about taxes, politicians and the President? When we look at the big picture we can see that God has blessed America, and we should stop and thank Him, but just like the nation of Israel in the wilderness, we only think of ourselves.

I often ponder on this time in my life and am still amazed how God led us to the very place where folks had just what we needed to continue our journey.

On occasion I find myself bellyaching about something that doesn't amount to a hill of beans for the Lord. It is at this time that I have to stop and look at the big picture of life. What is really going to matter five minutes after we are dead? Only that which is done for the Savior will have any true value in eternity.

As I started to repair the hitch, the rancher's wife came out to the bus and took Margie and the kids in the house for a pancake and sausage breakfast. Our kids got to watch their Saturday morning cartoons with the rancher's kids. As I was finishing up, the rancher returned. While we were talking he disclosed to me that he owned forty-four thousand acres of land. I couldn't comprehend one person owning all that land. He called it a ranch, and when I asked him why he, and his twelve- year old son, wore guns strapped to their leg, he said they wore them while out doing their chores for killing snakes and wolves. That place made me feel as though I were on location for a western movie.

We had breakfast together. I shared my faith in Jesus Christ with him and his family, but they were already Christians. An hour later we loaded up and pulled out fresh, with a new ray of hope that, yes, the Lord is still leading us to our destination.

We continued for the next two days. The weather had turned extra cold again, and we ran into patches of snow. One doesn't cover a lot of miles while driving fifty miles per hour. Our bus was like most buses, the heater only worked when it was warm outside. The kids were all bundled up in the blankets we had stacked on the mattresses.

One night we pulled into a little town. I think it was called Twin Forks. It was about nine o'clock when we found a motel, the only one in town, and settled in for the night. I told Margie, "Tomorrow we are going to make up for lost time, so we are going to get an early start."

The next morning we woke up approximately four-thirty. Margie peeked out the window and said, "You may as well go back to bed. There is a blizzard out there."

I responded, "No problem, we'll just drive out of it." I went out, scraped the ice off the windows on the bus, and started it up, hoping to get some heat.

We were soon all loaded up and ready to go. We pulled out of the motel parking area, and went one block where we were going to make a left turn onto a street that lead to the freeway. As I turned, I cut it too short and drove into a ditch. The back of the bus and the front of the Blazer were in the ditch. I told Margie to take the kids and go back to the motel room, but she said she had locked the keys in the room as we left.

I can remember getting out of the bus, walking down the street, and standing under the only street light in town, griping and complaining to the Lord. The snowflakes were about the size of a quarter, and the wind was blowing so hard that I could hardly remain standing. It was about five o'clock in the morning, the bus was stuck in the ditch, the wife and kids were freezing, and we were about a week and a half behind schedule. It was just another weight placed on me to make me stronger, and just like a weight lifter I would struggle with it until I could handle it, thus becoming a stronger Christian. I thought to myself, "How do I get into these situations? I don't get it.

I noticed a bread truck backed up to the only diner in town, so I went to the back door and explained the situation to the lady who owned the place. She told me to get my family and bring them in out of the weather. She said the gas station across the street would open at eight o'clock, and Sam, the owner, would be more than happy to help. I gathered up the family and took them to the diner where they ordered breakfast, but I was too antsy, so I went back out to the bus.

I prayed and asked the Lord to get me out of yet another mess. I started the bus and put it in gear, but nothing happened. I was so upset, I disconnected the Blazer and single-handedly pushed it out of the ditch. I climbed back into the bus and told the Lord, "Lord, if this is where this old bus breaks down, this is where we'll stay." I rocked the bus back and forth, back and forth, and the clutch started smoking. I could smell it burning. I was revving up the engine and rocking the bus back and forth. I probably woke everybody in town. The harder I tried, the angrier I became.

All of a sudden, as if the Lord was saying, "Okay, dummy," I'll bail you out one more time. The bus seemed to jump right out of the ditch. It happened so fast, I almost drove across the street to another ditch. I backed up the bus and hooked up the Blazer. By this time it was seven o'clock. I pulled in front of the diner, and as I turned off the engine I heard a pinging sound. I had heard that sound before. It was the water pump. The bearings were going out. If it isn't one thing, it's two!

I told Margie and the lady in the diner the bad news. The lady said that Sam would be in the gas station about eight o'clock, and he could fix anything. I had some time before Sam was due to arrive at the gas station, so I had breakfast and drank about a gallon of coffee. Eight o'clock finally rolled around and as we were sitting there we were looking out the window gazing across the street to where Sam's gas station was, waiting for Sam to show up. It got to be eight-ten, eight-twenty, and still no Sam. By this time I was becoming rather fidgety. At eight-thirty Sam finally pulled into the station. He jumped out of his truck and went inside. The lady in the diner used the phone to call Sam, but as we watched, it was obvious that Sam wasn't going to answer his phone.

I walked over to Sam's garage. I noticed that Sam had left his truck door open and the engine was still running. I introduced myself and said, "Sam, see that bus next door? The water pump is going out and I wonder if you can fix it?"

Sam didn't even look up as he gathered a bunch of tools and took them to his truck. He finally acknowledged my presence and said, "The garage is closed for today. I'm going to be mending fences all day." He then jumped in his truck and left.

By this time the snow had stopped and the wind had died down, so there I was, standing at a closed garage trying to figure out what to do next. I went back to the diner and told Margie and the lady what Sam had told me. Some of those towns are over one hundred miles apart; one doesn't just drive from one town to another in a matter of minutes. I told Margie we would drive the bus, until it quit, then take it from there.

It has been said that faith is idle when circumstances are right; only when they are adverse is one's faith in God exercised. Just like a weight lifter grows strong with added weights and exercise, so it is with our faith in God and our Christian walk.

119

I went to the counter to pay the lady for all the food we had consumed and for the coffee I had drank, but she said, "This one's on the house. Preacher, you've got enough troubles." She filled up our thermos bottle and gave the kids their pick of all the candy under the glass counter. As I look back on life, it is the little blessings along the way that keep us going for the Lord!

I have made a list of all the blessings we have received after becoming Christians. Even now I have to stop and look back on all the things God had done for us and thank Him, then look forward to the next blessing.

We drove that old yellow bus to Coeur d'Alene, Idaho, where a college buddy of mine had started a church about a year earlier. We stayed at his home for a couple of days to rest up. While we were there I took the time to look over my water pump problem. After a little investigation I realized it wasn't the water pump after all. There was an aluminum fan on the alternator; it had broken loose when the alternator broke off the wheel well in Indiana about two weeks earlier.

I was asked to preach in my buddy's church on Sunday afternoon. I had preached only two or three sermons in my life. When I had finished they took up an offering for us. We received two hundred and fifty dollars. Along with this was the two hundred dollars we had received from the preacher in Council Bluffs, Iowa, and the fifty dollars my high school basketball hero had given to us. All this money was just enough to pay for the two rear ends on the bus, plus labor.

When I look back on it all, I realize that the Lord was blessing our faithfulness in His service, and had provided the funds to help us keep on. We had become stronger in the Lord's work because of the weights we had to lift thus far. If we had discarded any of them, we would never be the strong Christians we were as at this time in our Christian walk.

B'HAM

We arrived in Bellingham, Washington, two and one half weeks and two thousand, six hundred and forty-one miles after we started. It is a beautiful city with a population of about fifty thousand people. It is nestled in the hills on the West Coast, and has its own bay leading out to the Pacific Ocean. It is one of America's best kept secrets. On a clear day one can see Mt. Baker with its snow capped peaks in the distance.

Now that we have arrived, what should we do next? I thought that the first thing I should do was to find a job. My last year in Bible college, my income was twenty-two thousand five hundred dollars. What I didn't know was that our first year in the ministry we would make a total of six thousand dollars. We found a place to rent seven miles out of Bellingham. After we were settled in for a week or so, I took that old yellow bus to a nearby Navy base where we sold it for two hundred dollars more than we paid for it.

When I was still in Bible college the superintendent, of the plant where I worked, gave me the name and phone number of a gentleman to call once we arrived in B'Ham. I called him and told him who had given me his number, and that I needed work. Once he had learned who had given me his name and phone number he hired me over the phone, no questions asked. What I didn't know was that it was one of the highest paying jobs in the area. The job was at the Arco Refinery. I was hired as a Pipefitter, earning fourteen dollars and fifty cents per hour.

The Arco Refinery is one of two refineries in that area used to refine crude oil brought down from Alaska. We were their first stop once they reached what they called "the lower forty-eight." Yes sir, it was quite a job; even though it was only part time, it would be a tremendous help over the next four years.

About every five, or six months the refinery would close down a section for revamping. At that time they would hire about fifty of us until the work was done, then they would lay us off. Five or six months later they would hire us all back again. The longest we would work would be two months.

My new boss took a liking to me right away, so he put me on the docks to work. When the ships came in, it was our job to get into the little boat and stretch a floating rubber guard around the perimeter of the ship; it was about a quarter mile in diameter. This floating rubber guard protruded from the water approximately two feet and was close to two feet below the surface. This was used to protect the bay from an oil spill if one occurred.

When I hired in I had to sign papers stating that I could be tested for drugs at any time during my employment. One day during lunchtime I was sitting in my car eating lunch. The lunchroom was always overcrowded during a "shutdown." As I returned from lunch I had to pass through a gate in a fence that surrounded the refinery. As I passed the guard shack I was handed an envelope and told to report to personnel immediately. While I was walking to personnel I thought to myself, "Now what have I done?"

When I arrived at the personnel office there were fourteen men already present, each holding an envelope. A few minutes, after I arrived, the boss came in and announced that we were all going to a nearby town for a drug test. Naturally some of the men protested. The regular employees were warned about this very thing three months earlier, giving them ample time to get what drugs they had in their system out. We all piled into two company vans. It was very quiet on the way to the clinic. We were all given a urinalysis test. If memory serves me correctly this was on a Friday. By Monday afternoon we had received the results of the test. Of us fifteen men who had taken the test, only three of us had passed it. Twelve men were fired. That afternoon I didn't have a lead-man, as he was one of those who had been terminated. Sad, but true, some of those men had worked there for eight years or more, but now they were unemployed.

This is a perfect example of the Lord's return. Throughout the Scriptures we are warned to be ready, for in such an hour as we thing not, the Son of Man cometh. We are told to watch and pray and to be busy about our Lord's business. Most people live their lives as though they will never have to face God, but the Bible states in Romans 14:12, *"So then each of us shall give account of himself to God."* These men at the refinery had been given ample warning, but they didn't take heed. So it will be when Jesus returns. Millions will be caught unaware. Many will be left behind to face the Antichrist, False Prophet, and the tribulation period. The following Sunday I preached a sermon on preparing to meet God, using what had happened at the refinery as an example.

When we had been in B'Ham for a month or so, we rented a family restaurant on the edge of town. It was there we would be holding our church services. People often asked why we didn't get in a church with people, pews, and a piano like normal people would. Isn't it amazing how life will turn on you? That was about the same I had said about my godly mother-in-law and father-in-law years earlier. If one would stop and think about it, every church in the world had to have a founder, a beginning. Someone had to lay the foundation, not only on the building, but also on the Christian faith. God uses different people in different ways, and this seemed to be the way He was leading us.

A week before our first meeting I spent hours and hours on the street passing out literature pertaining to our new church, and on how to get to Heaven. It was going to be the fastest growing church in the great northwest! We were told the great northwest was the most "un-churched" area in America. We found out later that it was a fact.

Finally the big day came. We had a piano but no one to play it. We met in a banquet room in that little restaurant; I had set up thirty chairs. I had a pulpit made, and I placed it up front overlooking the crowd, so I could tell them all about Jesus. I had taped the music of four or five songs on a cassette tape to use for our song service.

We arrived early that first Sunday. My wife would be working in the nursery for the first couple of weeks until we found a permanent nursery worker. We made a few last-minute arrangements. I had practiced my sermon on my family the night before. It was from the book of John, chapter three, *"Ye must be born again."* Midway through my sermon a man about twenty-five years of age walked in with a Bible under his arm. He almost scared me to death. People were here, now what? After the service the visitor came up to me and asked, "Is this your first service?" I replied, "Yes, sir."

He said, "You did a good job except for one thing." I thought to myself, just great a critic already. "You forgot to take up the offering," he said. I told him that the rest of the folks were my family, and I didn't want to embarrass him if he wasn't prepared for an offering. He took out his check-book and wrote out the church's very first offering.

The next day I went out to visit the flock, after all I was a real pastor now. I called on the fellow who had visited the church the day before. He told me that the only reason he came was because he had lost his drivers license for drinking and driving a couple of weeks before, so he walked the quarter of a mile to the restaurant. I told him that the only reason we didn't have more people in church was because people didn't know we were in town yet. He looked me in the eye and said, "People don't care you're in town either." Reality was beginning to settle in.

I can remember the time during the early stages of our ministry, life as a pastor was like riding a spiritual roller coaster. Because of my desire to reach folks for Christ, if the crowds were down, I was down both spiritually and emotionally. It was a drain on me both mentally and physically. I still believe a pastor should have the largest crowds he can get, but I have learned to do my best and let God do the rest. It is no sin to have a little church, only if it stays that way over the years, then a pastor may have to do some soul searching. All God really expects out of us, is to be faithful to the things of God.

Our third Sunday morning service we had a young couple visit our church service. I had led the lady to the Lord while on visitation a week earlier. Their names were Dave and Peggy Zollner, and they came faithfully from then on. Within a month we had about thirty people coming, most of who were friends and relatives of the Zollners.

One Sunday afternoon we all went up to a lake in the mountains, and had our first church picnic, and we baptized our first converts. It was a beautiful, hot August day. No one told me that the water in those lakes was ice cold from the snow melting higher up the mountain. I wanted to appear spiritual, but we didn't have any baptismal robes, so I wore a pair of dark blue work coveralls with a white shirt and tie. I don't know if I impressed anyone or not, but I'm sure the Lord was pleased with our efforts.

About our fifth week, on a Sunday, we pulled into the parking lot to get ready for the services. There was a U-haul truck backed up to the kitchen area. When we got out of our car the owner strolled over to me and said, "You won't be able to have service here this afternoon." I asked if there was a problem, and she answered, "No, we sold the restaurant and the new owners take over today." I thought to myself, thanks for the notice. I didn't know what to do next. It was one of those weights the Lord had put on me to make me stronger. It was all the weights I had struggled with along the

GETTING STRONGER

way which enabled me to be a strong enough Christian to handle this added weight. If I had shied away from the previous weights, I wouldn't have been able to handle this one.

We started looking for another place to meet immediately; if the Lord was in this thing I would do my best, and God would handle the rest. Within a couple of days we had found a beautiful, old, red, square-dance barn two miles from the restaurant. We made a bargain with the owner allowing us to paint the barn for the first three months rent. It was perfect. The upper loft where we held our services was finished in knotty pine and had an English hardwood floor, which had a high gloss shine to it. There was a kitchen downstairs and two restrooms for men and women.

I had promised Margie years before that if we ever graduated from Bible College we would attend the graduation exercises. When I graduated from Embry-Riddle Aeronautical University in Daytona Beach, Florida, we didn't attend the graduation exercises because I had found employment, and we had moved out of the area. Besides, Margie was seven months pregnant with our second daughter. So, a week before graduation we drove back to Indiana for graduation in May; we had finished our classes in January.

Along with graduation there were about ten of us who were going to be ordained. After we received our diplomas the ordination service began. I was to walk to the front of the massive auditorium of the First Baptist Church of Hammond and kneel near the altar. Dr. Jack Hyles laid his hands on my head and prayed that the Holy Spirit of God would lead me through life for the glory of God. What a moment! There was almost three times the size of my home- town. It was as if an entire aircraft carrier had come to see us ordained. If the boys back at Cameno's hamburger joint could see me now! The next day we headed back to our mission field, B'Ham.

WELCOME TO THE MINISTRY

We continued to hold services in that old square-dance barn. Eventually we had more people in our church spiritually eligible for baptism. When we baptized in those days the entire congregation would leave church together, and we would drive to a little pond behind the local K-Mart. We would refer to these converts as our "blue light specials." One day upon arriving for a baptismal service, we found a party of people fishing. It was obvious they had been there all night, having beer cans and whiskey bottles all over the place. I began looking for someone who might be in charge. When I located him I asked him if he would please remove two or three of their fishing poles.

He was sucking on a big, old, nasty cigar as he asked me what in the blankety-blank was going on. I looked him in the eye and told him, "We're going to baptize some folks in the name of God the Father, and the Son, and the Holy Ghost." I thought he was going to swallow that cigar. He finally gave the command, and a couple of his cronies removed the fishing poles near the gravel boat ramp. Before we baptized we sang, "Shall We Gather at the River?" When we finished baptizing we gathered around and had a closing prayer. I can still see that fellow in my mind's eye with his cigar in his mouth, and as we were pulling out he was scratching his head as if to say, "What's going on?"

There was a family in the church who said, if we ever located anyone who could play an organ they would donate one to the church. I would get so frustrated with the tape recorder for music; we would have two verses to each song and then a pause. If we had a good crowd I would get all excited and would sing three verses of a song. It was like a three- ring circus at times, as we would be singing the third verse of Amazing Grace to the music of Victory in Jesus. As I look back on those days, it is quite clear that it was the Lord who was getting all the glory, not man.

One day, while visiting in the community, I met a man who told me he was praying about a place to serve the Lord. He told me that he played the piano. After I explained to him the situation of our church, he said he would be happy to play the organ for us. So, late that Saturday night we moved the organ into the square-dance barn. The next morning the organ player and his wife arrived at the square-dance barn extra early to get the feel of the instrument. He was playing the organ as the people were arriving. When they heard the music, they asked if we had a new tape. It was yet another answer to prayer. Within a month the church was given a piano.

During this time we had a young family in our church traveling over forty miles every service to be with us. They eventually moved to Bellingham. They were Bill and Janeece Talbot and their daughter, Janeene. Bill played the trumpet and his wife played an electric guitar. Between our piano player and the Talbot's we had some outstanding music in our church services.

After attending our church for awhile, Bill became burdened for lost souls who were perishing without Jesus Christ. The Bible states in Proverbs 11:30, *"The fruit of the righteous is a tree of life; and he that winneth souls is wise."* The fruit of an apple tree is apples, the fruit of an orange tree is oranges, and this the Scripture teaches that the fruit of a Christian should be other Christians.

Bill thought it strange, as did I, when President John F. Kennedy was shot in 1963, by means of radio and television, people on the other side of the world knew of his death within two hours, and ninety percent of the world learned of his death within twenty-four hours. The worst failure of the Christian is that nearly two thousand years have passed since Jesus died on the cross to provide salvation for the world, and millions upon millions do not know of it.

Bill asked me to teach him how to win someone to Christ. What an honor it is to teach someone how to lead someone to the Savior! I gave him some literature to study and told him that when he thought he was ready, to let me know and he could go with me into God's vineyard. I would go from door to door telling people about our new church and the Lord.

After a month of studying the literature I had given him, Bill informed me that he thought he was ready to go door to door with me. I was more excited about his burden than he was. I told him we would do some survey work in one of the more quiet areas on Saturday. It was a beautiful day, the sun was shining, and just a little breeze made it a perfect day. People were out in their yards working in their flower- beds or just stretched out on their lawn chairs; just enjoying the day. We went to several homes and, as usual, on a pleasant day people were extra kind to us.

This is what I enjoy the most; every door is a new adventure and opportunity to be a witness for Jesus Christ. Bill seemed to be enjoying himself, so after about half an hour I asked him to take the next door. Bill rang the doorbell, and a little fellow answered the door looking to be about twenty-five years of age wearing just a pair of sweat pants. Bill looked him in the eye, told him his name, and introduced me. The fellow began yelling, "I'm an Atheist, I'm an Atheist." Bill was concentrating so hard on what he was going to say next that he didn't pay any attention to what the guy was saying.

Bill then said, "Sir, do you go to church anywhere?" This fellow literally jumped up and down yelling at the top of his lungs, "I'm an Atheist, I'm an Atheist." Again, Bill paid him no mind as he asked him, "If you were to die today do you know if you would go to Heaven?"

By this time the little fellow was going crazy and was cursing us like dogs. I figured things had gone far enough, and I am afraid I got in the flesh as I told the fellow that if we were on the sidewalk he wouldn't talk like he was doing. I have confessed this sin of pride to the Lord many times since then. As we were walking across this guy's yard to the sidewalk I asked myself, "What would the Apostle Paul do in a spot like this?" When we reached the sidewalk that little wild man took a karate stance.

I soon gathered my composure and said, "Hold the phone man, all we want to do is give you an invitation to church." The atheist was a fool because according to the Bible in Psalm 14:1 it states, *"The fool hath said in his heart there is no God."* He jumped up on the hood of a car in front of his house and started singing, "Jesus—the little children, all the children of the world, Jesus—the little children, all the children under three." By this time all the people who were out in their yards started gathering their children up and taking them into their homes. People were taking up their lawn chairs and going inside. We could still hear him singing his disgusting song a block away.

Bill said to me a little later that day, "Pastor, I don't think I'm cut out for this soul-winning business." After what we experienced earlier I didn't know if I was either! A month had gone by and Bill came to me and said he would like to try soul winning again. I told him of the thousands of doors I had knocked on and that kind of thing had never happened before, and it would probably never happen again. That had been Bill's first door, and I have to admit, I didn't think he would try again.

Bill had a broken heart for lost souls. When God breaks one's heart to do something for Him, they won't quit at the first obstacle. I become a little concerned about people who are going into the ministry, and then a year later they are selling insurance. A lot of Bible college, students are momma-called and daddy-sent, not God-called or God-sent.

Several months went by, and the Talbot's decided to move into the Se-attle area. The last time I talked to them they were heading up a soul-winning program in a large church where they were attending. Bill told me that he had taught ten people how to win souls, and those ten were teaching others to do likewise. God isn't looking for mighty men, He is looking for faithful men. The Bible states in II Timothy 2:2, *"And the things that thou hast heard of me among many witnesses, the same commit thou to faithful men, who shall be able to teach others also."*

We stayed in that old, red, square dance barn all of our first winter. We had to find another place to baptize because of the cold weather. One of the fellows in the church had a friend who had a sauna in a shed in his back yard. One cold, snowy, January day we gathered around that little shed and sang, "Shall We Gather at the River" and baptized some new converts. Someone had taken a picture of me baptizing these folks in the sauna. There I was with my dark blue coveralls, white shirt and tie, and in the back-ground were half a dozen empty Budweiser bottles. I didn't look very spiritual, but it did remind me of how good God had been to me over the last six years.

Our first Halloween in B'Ham was on a Sunday, so I thought I would try to have a special service that day. I called one of the local morticians and asked if our church could "borrow" a casket. He told me that if he allowed us to borrow one, he would have to let every college kid in town borrow one. He said, "Reverend, if you want to you can use our funeral home that day free of charge." I believed that was a great idea, so I told the folks in our church that we were going to have a special day on Halloween Sunday, and that they were supposed to invite as many people as possible for this surprise event.

Every Sunday, I would remind them of our special Halloween service.

Finally, on Halloween Sunday morning, I told the folks to rendezvous with my wife at McDonald's and she would lead them to our special meeting place.

I arrived at the funeral home early and put the casket up front. I was wearing my black suit and black tie. Margie had put some makeup on my face to make me look much older, a lot paler; I looked pretty spooky. The folks followed Margie into the parking lot. It was a record attendance. I didn't crack a smile as they entered and went into the main chapel where our organist was playing some typical eerie music. They went in and sat down, and were cutting up and laughing. I called one of the men over and told him to tell them to have some respect for the dead. I must have been convincing because he went in and quieted the crowd.

The casket was closed, so no one knew if there was a body in it or not. As I look back on this event, I may have overdone it just a little; I'm surprised someone didn't walk out of the proceedings. I went into the chapel area, went up to the front, took out a big, black family Bible, and preached a sermon on "Prepare to meet thy God!" I kept referring to the casket and saying things like; this person had only one chance to serve the Lord, now his chance is gone, or, this person will never again be able to tell anyone how to become a true Christian. I told them repeatedly that they should serve the Lord now, while they had their health and faculties, because the day would come when they will become the guest-of-honor at a funeral home somewhere.

When I had finished preaching I had the congregation to stand and form a line on one side of the chapel. I told them that we were going to "view the body." They looked at one another as if to say, "View what body?" I opened the casket lid, and one by one they went by and looked inside the casket. I had propped a mirror on a pillow at the head of the casket, and when the folks looked inside they saw themselves. It was a week or so later that I was told I had offended some of the people who had attended. They said I was a heretic, just another Jim Jones. I may not have used a lot of wisdom with my zeal, but this I do know, they got the message. The Bible states in James 4:14, *"For what is your life? It is even a vapor, that appeareth for a little time, and then vanisheth away."* If you (reader) have been lackadaisical about your Christian service, please, for Jesus' sake, get off your blessed assurance and become a productive Christian!

That Halloween service reminded me of the time I worked at Allis-Chalmers in Indiana as an unsaved pipefitter. One day at lunchtime four or five men jumped on their motorcycles to rush down to McDonald's two blocks away. On their return to work one of the men's helmet fell off the backrest of his seat. The helmet bounced off the asphalt and into the lake next to the road. He turned around, parked his motorcycle, and went to fetch his helmet. By this time his buddies had turned around and were laughing at him. As he bent over to retrieve his helmet it floated out of his reach, so he pulled off his shoes and waded out to get it. The closer he got to his helmet, the further it floated out. When he was almost up to his knees in the water he fell into a hole. They didn't find him for almost three hours. His mother, father, sister, and two brothers also worked at the plant. What a tough job it was for those who had to call to the office all those folks, and tell them that their loved- one had just drowned at lunchtime. It was another reminder that we have no promises of tomorrow!

After having met approximately a year in the square-dance barn, the dear lady who owned it passed away. Her son-in-law, the politician, doubled the rent on us a week later. Needless to say, we began looking for another place to meet. Even though we were still struggling financially as a church, it seemed as though the Lord always made a way. This incident was just another weight placed on me to help me become a stronger Christian. It seemed as though I was getting pretty good at handling this kind of pressure, only because I took these burdens one at a time.

I finally found what appeared to be an old abandoned fire station, which was located in town off from the main street. When I inquired about the building I learned that it belonged to a lodge. The lodge members were remodeling the building. After a couple of meetings with the president of the lodge we struck a deal. For every twenty adult man-hours we worked on their building we would get in return one month of free rent. We had been meeting in the building for a couple of months when we had some crafts-men from a church in Seattle and Abbotsford, British Columbia, in Canada come to help with the project. Within months we had finished their lodge and had earned two and one half years of free rent; what a blessing!

HELP OR HINDRANCE

A few weeks after arriving in Washington I had received a letter from a church in Olympia. I didn't know anyone from that area. I opened the letter and found a check for one hundred dollars. The attached note read, "Welcome to God's country." When someone sends you a hundred dollars you are motivated to meet that person.

One day I was invited to a fellowship meeting, for pastors and their families, and it was there I met Richard Hill. As it turned out, we had more people in church than he did. The Lord had laid it on his heart to send me a hundred dollars, and I felt led to accept it. Richard Hill was a good looking, older man, the athletic type. He was the kind of guy who kept every one of his blonde hairs in place.

I had kept in touch with Richard over the years. He had started the Calvary Church years before and was still struggling. One day he called me and told me that he had been voted in as pastor of a good-sized church in Portland, Oregon. He invited us down and showed off his building, and Christian school. I thought to myself, "The Lord has blessed his faithfulness."

Six months later I received a call from Richard. It was on a Wednesday evening, and we were having Bible study in our home, because the building we used for our Sunday services was being utilized during the week. He called and asked how things were going. I told him we were being faithful and doing the best we could. Usually when a preacher makes that statement the crowds are down, the offerings are down, and the preacher is down.

Richard told me that he wanted to move to Bellingham and help us with our church. I said, "I thought you were set for life where you are." He told me something had come up, and he thought it would be a good idea to get away for awhile. It was a fact that we were struggling, just like any new church would, and it sounded like a good idea to have someone help out a little. After all, I was working a forty-hour a week job and didn't have time to minister to the folks like I should. I asked Richard, "Why do you feel you should move?"

He answered, "There was a conflict with some of the folks in the church, and I don't think it will work out." He told me that some of the parents were upset with him because of the way he had handled a discipline problem with one of the students. I always was a soft touch for a sob story.

As always, I was for the underdog, so I told him he could move up with us until it all blew over. I asked him when they (his wife and three teenagers) wanted to move up, and he said that very night. I thought that was rather fast, but I also thought about that one hundred dollars he had sent to a preacher he had never met before. He asked if we could drive down and pick them up because his car was broken down, and he didn't know how to repair it. I told him they could stay with us until they found a house to rent. When our conversation ended we took up an offering for gas so we could go down and fetch this family.

Richard told me it wouldn't be any problem for him and his wife to find employment. He had worked for a newspaper in Olympia, and his wife had worked in a bank. I felt this was the break we had been waiting for. This guy had a nice singing voice. I could appoint him as song leader; and with his children, and mine, we could have a children's, choir. I had big plans!

My parents had sent us an Atari game for Christmas, and I held the Pac-man record at some twelve thousand points. I told Richard and his family they were welcome to stay, but if they broke my record in Pac-man they would have to leave. Two weeks later neither one of them had gotten a job or even started looking for work. Besides that, after playing Pac-man for two weeks all day long, the new record was one hundred and twenty-five thousand. I mentioned to Richard about his getting a job, and the next day he found his kids a job delivering newspapers. This helped, but not enough. I learned one thing fast, teenagers can eat you out of house and home.

I was working in a garage where I worked on sports cars. It was like working on roller skates, as I was bent over those little cars all day long. This was one of those periods that I was laid off from the Arco Refinery. I would go home for lunch smelling like a grease pit and with an aching back, and they would be waiting patiently for me to pull in so they could eat. After having been there for a month, this guy hadn't done a thing to further the progress of the church, and naturally, because he didn't have a job, he didn't contribute financially either.

Finally, after two and one-half months, with all my dreams and expectations gone, I realized I was going to have to make a move. I think the thing that hit me the hardest was when, after every Sunday morning service, having preached my heart out, he would belittle me. While we were eating the food I had paid for and my wife had prepared, in the house where I paid the rent, he would correct me on my pronunciation of some of the words in my sermon, and he did this in front of my children. He would say things such as, "in the original Greek," or he would give us some long, drawn out doctrinal statement to back himself up. It has been said the Devil has no great interest in destroying the church, he would rather run it. Richard and his family had run our phone bill up to over one hundred dollars.

One day I came home for lunch, and there they all were standing in line waiting for me to get home so they could chow down. Richard said half jokingly, "It's about time!" That did it! I was in one of those hot Italian moods anyway. I asked him to step outside where I told him in Christian love, "Either you get a job, or you'll have to leave."

He said, "I'll send my wife out looking for a job tomorrow." I replied, "Forget about your wife, you need to get a job!" He looked at me with big, sad eyes and said, "But Brother Delli, the last time we moved in with someone it was eight months before my wife found a job." I thought I was going to have a heart attack when I heard that.

It was an added weight that was placed on me. Even though I had handled the burden up until now, it was a strain. I know the Lord allowed the added pressure to help me become a stronger Christian, but it was quite a load. Just like a weight lifter never gets stronger unless he keeps adding weights, so it is in the Christian life; the more the weight, the stronger the Christian. I wanted to become stronger, so I agonized with it until I could handle it.

When I came home that afternoon from work, Richard and his family, along with all their belongings, were gone. I asked Margie where everybody was, and she said, "I don't know what you said to Richard at noon today, but you should have said it two months ago." They had packed up and headed out, just like I said they could if they weren't willing to contribute.

It is sad, but true, there are people in the ministry, just like any other profession, who are nothing more than bums, professional bums. The Bible states that if you don't work, you don't eat! Our society says otherwise with all the financial aid programs going on in America. It is a wonder anybody works anymore. We have taught our children in America that all you have to do is have four or five illegitimate children, and Uncle Sam will give you so much money for each one. You will get special housing, food stamps, and just about anything else you want, as long as you don't get married or get a job. Several of these programs have people on them who

GETTING STRONGER

are healthy, intelligent individuals who, if they had to work for a living, would make a decent wage, but would lose all their benefits, so why bother to work? I often marvel how generation, after generation in America are becoming more and more dependent on the government to meet their needs, rather than themselves. If we destroy the work ethic in America, we'll eventually destroy this great nation God has put us in. In America, government has lost its credibility, business has lost its integrity, hard work has lost its dignity, morality has lost its nobility, and worst of all, true Christianity has lost its vitality. People want more for doing less, and ethical standards are no longer fashionable. There is one discouraging thing about the rules of success – they don't work unless we do.

Approximately a month later I received a phone call from Richard Hill, telling me they moved to Seattle and that the Salvation Army had put them up for the first week. From there they were led to some kind of financial assistance program, then they were placed in a brand new condominium overlooking Puget Sound. He told me that his wife had finally found a job (this con-artist had done it again!) I wonder how his children are going to turn out after watching this smooth talking bum in action all their lives.

You may be asking yourself, "Could Richard Hill be a real Christian?" We must remember that salvation brings eternal life, not character. If a bum gets saved, he is going to stay a bum unless he gets under the preaching and teaching of the Word of God. It is the principles of the Bible that bring character, but only if we apply them to our lives. Character is doing right regardless if anybody is watching or not. If we stop and think for a moment, I am sure we have run across a Richard Hill in most of our lives.

THE LAST STRAW

We held our services in that old, converted fire hall for almost a year after we had completed all of the remodeling. One day a lodge member came to me with a complaint about our children bothering the liquor in their bar room, which was our nursery area, so they locked us out of there. They also locked us out of our junior church area with some other lame excuse. It was obvious what was happening; we had worked and gotten their hall looking real nice, but now that the work was all done we had served our usefulness to them. I was expecting them to lock us out of the restrooms next. It didn't seem right for them to push us out, after all the work we had done for them. By the time they had finished, the only place we had was the main auditorium. No more nursery, no more junior church, no more reason to stay!

It was a decision I had to make. Free rent or no free rent, it was time to get out from under the thumbs of those unconverted lodge members. Although we had over a year and a half of free rent still due us, we decided to make a move. As I recall our services in that lodge hall, I realize we didn't have the response to the preaching of God's Word that we had in that old, red barn.

It was about this time that I was introduced to a preacher who had some experience in church planting from down south. One day I gave him a call and arranged to meet him at the local McDonalds. I picked his brain for almost an hour. He was much younger than I had first thought him to be.

Dr. Jack Hyles once said, "Every man knows something that I do not know. I must find what it is and learn it. Hence, all men are my teachers." I took Charlie Lee over to our new meeting place. It was a landmark, one of the oldest buildings in town. It was a beautiful, old building in the old section of town. From the top floor one could look out over Bellingham Bay with its islands. The site was breathtaking, especially at sunset. The building had a kitchen area, and a large room in which made a nice nursery. Our piano player loved it because it had a nice baby grand piano in the main hall. Yes, we had come a long way since that family restaurant and tape recorder.

Charlie Lee gave me some advice about seating arrangements and a few other things, and informed me that he would call me in a couple of weeks. Within a month he called me and asked if he could come up and preach for us on a Sunday morning, and I said that would be just fine. When he arrived I introduced him to some of the men. He gave us the impression that he had access to a large sum of money to help such a work as ours. Once again, I became excited. Was this an answer to prayer? Although he never mentioned a figure, it sounded good to me; after all, I was sick and tired of working all those rotten jobs to support my family and the church. We had been there approximately three years, but we had moved meeting places as many times, and each time we moved we lost some folks. We now had a respectable building, a baby grand piano, a fair core of people, and now a ray of hope, some financial backing.

Charlie Lee said he would be willing to move up to the area and help out. The first question I asked him, "Are you going to rent or buy a house?" After the Richard Hill experience I wanted to get that part clear before he moved. A little over a month later he moved to Bellingham. He told me he would like to preach at least once a week, and I told him that wouldn't be a problem. Five weeks later his wife joined him.

Charlie bought a fine house in the Bellingham area. He had two campers and drove a Cadillac. Within a month Charlie had his sister and brother-in-law, who was a preacher also, move to the area, then his two cousins moved in also. His sister played the piano, his wife sang, and his brother-in-law preached. Before I realized what was happening, I wasn't even in the picture anymore. There were Sundays when I came to church that Charlie and his kronies didn't even speak to me. He would take notes while I was preaching, but I learned later that he was criticizing my sermons, then explaining to his relatives how it should be done correctly.

I admit that I am not the world's greatest orator, but souls were still coming to the Savior regardless of my mistakes. One would have thought that I would have learned my lesson by now. Charlie's way of reasoning was, if one had a lot of things, then God was blessing him; it's called prosperity theology. Prosperity theology is Humanism cloaked in theological terminology. It is a mockery of God and reduces Him to a giant "Santa Claus" in the sky. Push the right button and God will give you what you want. Like Humanism it makes man and his needs the center of the universe. It forces God to become the servant of man. Prosperity theology is not scriptural. The Apostle Paul is proof of that, and the Lord didn't even have a pillow for His head. Charlie would walk over to his black Cadillac and say, "Look how God has blessed me." True Christianity, like true love, is to give, and give, and give, expecting nothing in return. When a person gives to get, their motive is wrong. The Bible states that man looketh on the outward appearance, but the Lord looks on the heart. It is true that God may bless a person for their efforts, but if He doesn't, that is not proof they are a second-class Christian.

One Sunday morning after church, as was the custom, my wife and I stayed behind to clean up for the evening service. As we were cleaning up, Margie found a Bible on one of the chairs. As she thumbed through it, to find out whom it belonged to, she discovered a piece of paper. It was Charlie's Bible, and on the paper was a list of all the things wrong with our ministry, including accusing me of using church money for personal use. The list was quite long; it also listed all the things wrong with me, and my family. There were other accusations about my inability to preach, my lack of love, and my unwillingness to share my pulpit. Margie broke down and began weeping uncontrollably. It was too much for her. Finally she said, "He is going to destroy everything we've worked for over these years." I was afraid she was right. As I recall, the only people in our church contributing financially were Dave Zollner (my deacon) and myself.

Yes, it was a heavy, heavy weight placed upon my wife and I. I honestly didn't know if we could handle it. It was just like a weight lifter, after he has lifted weights for some time, keeps adding weights to make himself stronger, but even a weight lifter reaches his limit. I had burdens placed on me from the second day I became a Christian, and each time I accepted more burdens, more weights, hoping to become a stronger Christian, but I may have reached my limit.

I prayed and asked the Lord to help me through this time, then I went home and called Charlie Lee. I told him I wanted to buy him a cup of coffee, and that I would meet him in a little café out in the country near his house. I sat down across from him and said, "This relationship we have in the church is like a marriage. We need to keep the lines of communication open." As he gave me one of his big smiles, he said in his Southern drawl, "That's right Pastor, whatever you say."

About that time I pulled out that despicable list and held it under his nose. "Maybe we can start with this," I said. His eyes bulged and he started spitting and sputtering, then he tried to grab the list out of my hand, saying it was his personal property. If something like this would have happened in my Navy days, I would have decked him, but God has helped me with my quick Italian temper that I inherited from my dad. I told Charlie, "It's your list, but my name is written all over it."

GETTING STRONGER

I could just see the gears turning in his pea brain as he was trying to think of some way to lie his way out of this predicament. For the next fifteen minutes I read him the riot act (in Christian love of course). He eventually looked at me and said, "Pastor, that was a prayer list. I was praying for you in those areas." Sad, but true, not everyone in the ministry is motivated by the things of God.

Our nation has had her eyes opened to some wolves in sheep's clothing, starting with the impeachment of ex-president Nixon, the Bakkers, and Jimmy Swaggert, and in recent weeks Martin Luther King, Jr. has been proven guilty of plagiarism. We may never know of all those who have destroyed the trust of the American people in places of leadership. For every Charlie Lee there are thousands of men and women dedicated to glorifying God through their loyalty and commitment to His cause. These folks are winning others to Christ and displaying the true meaning of Christianity. Sad, but true, the world uses these false prophets as examples for Christianity, but remember, the Lord Jesus is keeping score, not man.

I was working yet another job in a little machine shop some twenty miles away. I could feel myself becoming run-down. With work, the church, and the problems along the way, I was becoming physically worn out. There were times during this period that I would break down and begin to weep for no apparent reason. Sunday around our house was becoming the most miserable day of the week. Every time I would enter the pulpit to speak I had to watch all my p's and q's to avoid being accused of something falsely. My children knew when it was Sunday, because I would always be in a bad mood. I had done something I had promised I wouldn't do; I had allowed the circumstances to interfere with my home life and my preaching.

I began asking myself if I had made a mistake by coming out west. Had I made a blunder going into the ministry? These are the thoughts that ran through my mind often during that time. This one thing I did know, I was saved and on my way to Heaven, and I was going to do everything in my power to take others with me. I sometimes wonder how many preachers have been where I was during those difficult days. Maybe you're reading this book and someone has turned on you. Maybe you have a broken heart. Let me assure you, it will be worth it all when we see Jesus. Booker T. Washington once said, "Success is to be measured, not so much by the position that one has reached in life, as by the obstacles which he has overcome while trying to succeed."

If you are under a burden, under a weight, wrestle with it until you get the victory, and you will become stronger in the work of the Lord. Keep on keeping on for the Lord. There are better days ahead. There are sunny days that want to shine on you. There are rewards waiting for you in glory. Hang tough, don't quit, and just keep looking up.

One day, I had some visitors who drove up from Seattle, they were Dr. Ken Blue and Dr. Eugene Kimmel. Now, here were a couple guys who had accomplished in their ministry what I wanted to accomplish in mine. They took me out for dinner, asked me about the church, and how my wife felt about the ministry and the people. We went for a ride in the mountains. It was a relaxing time for me to know that these busy men would take time for me. After they had left I said to Margie, "I wonder what they wanted." They had more worthwhile things to do with their time.

Approximately a month later I received a call from Dr. Blue. He offered me a job as an associate pastor with a full-time salary. At first I thought it might have been a joke, but then I realized this was God's way of repaying our faithfulness. Before I had hung up the phone, I knew that I would take the position. I thought to myself, if Charlie Lee and his relatives wanted our church so badly they could have it. So, after four years and one month on this mission field, it was time for us to move on. Now I know why Dr. Blue and Dr. Kimmel spent the day with me; they were checking me out to see if I had any bitterness in my heart toward the ministry. I must have passed the test. Just think, I wouldn't have to work any more of those rotten jobs.

One of the loneliest days of my life was the day I backed a U-haul truck up to our back door. As I loaded it all by myself I thought, "Where is the flock? Where are all the people we lead to the Lord? Where are the folks we prayed for and cried over and poured our lives for, where are they? Where are the folks who we taught about the Lord? Where are all the folks we helped feed and found jobs for while we've been here these years?"

Dr. Jack Hyles once said, "If you have won the right to know how it feels to lose, your entire ministry will be wrapped up in making winners out of losers." This would have been the height of failure if we merely served mankind; this indeed would have been a poor recompense. It is to my joy that I serve Him who never fails to reward His servants to the full extent of His promises, if not here, then on the other side of glory!

It dawned on me, "This is what happened to Jesus as He was hanging on the cross. Where were all the people He had healed? Where were the blind He made to see, the lame that could walk, the lepers who were cleanses? Where were the five thousand that were fed, and where were His disciples whom He had loved and taught?" Then for the first time in my life I realized how much Jesus really loved me. As I loaded our last appliance on that U-haul, I prayed and asked the Lord to forgive me for having a pity party, and thanked Him for the souls He had given us in this place.

A BREATH OF FRESH AIR

The church in Seattle was a large church. It had a high attendance day of over eighteen hundred. They had more people in church than we had in my hometown. The church paid for the U-haul and gas to help us make the move. They even had people unload it when we arrived. It was like a breath of fresh air, a brook in the way, an oasis.

My first day on the job I arrived early. It was a Monday, and the rest of the staff had the day off. Pastor Blue and I went into the pastor's study; the carpeting was so thick that if one didn't pick their feet up they would trip. He sat me down and bragged on me for fifteen minutes, then he said, "I have a job that needs to be taken care of right away."

I sat up straight and thought to myself, "This is more like it. Here I am, a staff member of one of the largest independent, Baptist churches in the entire state of Washington." I was eagerly awaiting my first assignment.

Dr. Blue looked me in the eye and said, "Here it is. I want you to go down to the ladies restroom, to the third stall, and repair the wall divider." I looked him right back in the eye and said, "Yes sir," and I went and completed the assignment. Months later, after I had proven myself worthy, I was given more spiritual responsibilities. Dr. Blue told me that if I had, on my first assignment, hesitated even a little, he could not have used me. He said, "There is no room for pride in the Lord's work."

On Friday I was a pastor, and on the following Monday I was the janitor. Never once did I question God for placing me in that church. I was there because God had found me faithful. All He expects out of us is to be faithful. Not everyone can be a pastor, or play the piano, but all of us can be faithful. When I stand before the Lord I want Him to say to me, "*Well done, good and faithful servant; thou hast been faithful over a few things, I will make thee ruler over many things: enter thou into the joy of Thy Lord.*" That verse is found in Matthew 25:23.

Besides being the all-around fit-it man at the church, I had other responsibilities. I was given a list of about fifty people who were carpenters, painters, mechanics, electricians and plumbers. This was something new for me. When I was a pastor, if anything was broken, I was the one who had to figure out how to fix it.

Dr. Blue had started a building program on an educational building. When completed, it would be worth somewhere in the neighborhood of three-quarters of a million dollars. This was a real learning experience, working with different tradesmen. It was quite a blessing to see people willing to use their talents in the Lord's work, unlike in a struggling new church like I was accustomed to, where we had to give things away just to get people to show up, let alone do anything once they got there.

My very first Monday on my new job I was downstairs doing some work, when I saw a fellow coming out of one of the rooms. Being new, I didn't know who he was, so I introduced myself to him.

He said that he had lost his prescription sunglasses the day before at the church, and he was looking for them. I took down his name and telephone number and told him that if I found his glasses I would give him a call. He was a young man, well dressed, and quite mannerly. I thought he was one of the members. After he left it dawned on me that all the doors were locked, so how did he get in? I went into the room I had seen him come out of, and sure enough, the window had been removed from the outside, and there were three electric typewriters sitting next to the opening. After further investigation, we found that he had things hidden in the bushes.

On Tuesdays we had our staff meetings. To me these meetings were most profitable. We would talk over church problems and make decisions on how to handle them. Dr. Blue gave us many books on leadership, which we went over chapter by chapter each week. My Wednesdays started at eight in the morning and lasted until about nine at night, or until after Bible study. Thursdays began at eight in the morning and lasted until about nine-thirty at night, or until after visitation. Fridays were my day off! Saturdays were from eight in the morning to about five in the afternoon. We had bus visitation, and things had to be gotten ready for Sunday services. My Sundays started about seven-thirty. I was in charge of a fleet of eight buses, so I had to be there to see that they got off on time. Sundays lasted until after church on Sunday night, which was somewhere between nine and ten o'clock (it was my responsibility to lock the doors, make sure lights were off, and set the alarm system). It's been said that if you want a forty-hour paycheck, work a forty-hour week! Amy Carmichael once said, "We have all eternity to celebrate the victories, but only a few hours before sunset to win them."

I was also put in charge of junior church, where we had between two and two hundred-fifty children every Sunday. There were ten to twelve adults who worked in junior church. For the most part, they were the most faithful people in the entire church.

As I recall, Pastor Blue started this great church some eighteen years earlier in his living room. The only people who attended his first meeting were his wife, Joyce, and their five children. What an encouragement!

We found out in a hurry that the big city life had its drawbacks. Our rent in Bellingham had been three hundred dollars per month. Here we paid six hundred dollars per month for a duplex apartment. Finances were tight, even though I was receiving a good salary and gas allowance.

EASTWARD WOE

Pastor Blue had informed me that he had a policy that none of his staff members would be allowed to preach. I knew about that policy when I hired in, but I didn't think it would bother me. After awhile I dreamed of a chance to be turned loose with one of my best outlines. Dr. Blue had seen my kind before. He often hesitated in hiring men who had been called to preach. Usually after about two years, they were ready to get back at it, as was my case. He understood completely, and I was glad. After looking for a church to pastor in Washington, we heard of one in our home state of Indiana. I made several phone calls and set up a date where I could preach and share my vision with the church in need of a pastor.

To show his gratitude for our efforts in the church, Pastor Blue gave us a Sunday school bus. It was blue and white, just like the one that pulled up in front of our house back in 1975 before I became a Christian. It had a picture of Mickey Mouse painted near the side door. We took all the seats out of it except for the front four, just like our trip out west. This time I had a good friend, who was an ace mechanic by the name of Dick Kimble, work on the bus for a week before we ventured across America again. Also, I had a trailer hitch made by someone who knew what he was doing. The night before we left, the church threw us a going away party. They passed the hat and gave us almost eight hundred dollars to get us out of town.

As I recall, it was raining the day we left. As a matter of fact, it rained the week we left. There we were with our blue and white bus, with Mickey Mouse painted on the side, and a black, Ford station wagon hooked up to the back. Dick Kimble was there when we were ready to leave, and we had a word of prayer together.

As we were driving down I-5 toward downtown Seattle, I wondered if it was all in vain, all the heartaches and trouble over the last six years in the great Northwest. Then I remembered the hundreds of people I had been with as they bowed their heads and prayed the sinner's prayer: "God have mercy on me a sinner." The folks who had won their first soul to Christ, and the Christians who had grown in the grace and knowledge of the Lord. Then I had a peace about me, knowing we had done our best for the Lord.

We drove into the heart of Seattle and were on I-5 just across from Boeing when the bus stopped; I mean everything went dead. We coasted over to the edge of the freeway. It was still raining when I climbed out of the bus and popped the hood. Everything seemed to look all right, but nothing worked, no lights, no windshield wipers, no heater, nothing! The traffic was speeding by as I looked out the window and thought to myself, "Here we go again." But I didn't let it get the best of me. I was strong enough to handle it without any panic. After all, I had been weight lifting for the last twelve years, and this was a piece of cake. I prayed and asked the Lord to bail me out of yet another mess.

I took the battery out of the Ford wagon and installed it in the bus, then I climbed in, turned the starter, and it started immediately. The kids were six years older by this time, and they were excited about this adventure across America. We had been on the road for nearly half an hour when I asked Margie, "What is that awful smell?" The bus had smoke in it, but everything seemed normal. After we had traveled for about a hundred miles we stopped to gas up the bus, and it was then I discovered what the burning smell was. It was the emergency brake. It had been in the "on" position for close to two hours. Needless to say, we didn't have an emergency brake after that! I checked the oil, and we were exactly four quarts low. I knew then that it was going to be an interesting trip, to say the least. Luckily, Dick Kimble had put five gallons of used oil in the back of the bus. If things continued as they were, that might be enough to get us out of the state of Washington.

Overall, it was a good trip. We had some extra money for motels and food, thanks to the folks at the church. Everything was going pretty well, except for the oil situation. Even though it did get a lot better as we traveled, it still took ten gallons to cross America to Indiana. Because we didn't have an emergency brake, I found a short ten-by-ten piece of lumber that we would put under the wheel when stopped on a hill. We pulled out of Laramie, Wyoming, early one morning going east on U.S. 80. There is one last mountain to climb before coming to the plains. We were crawling up the incline at about five miles per hour. It took almost forty-five minutes before we reached the summit.

As we reached the top, we heard this terrible noise coming from under the hood, and at the same time everything went dead. As I recall, it was about seven o'clock in the morning, and the air still had a nip in it from the night before. We coasted over to the side. I told Margie to get out and block the wheels with a block of wood. As I looked the situation over I noticed something lying in the middle of the freeway about a quarter of a mile back. I ran back to see what it was. It was our battery and it had fallen clean out of the bus. It was a miracle that we didn't run over it with the bus or the station wagon. By all rights it should have shattered into a million pieces. I looked it over, wired it back in the bus, climbed in the bus, started it up, and off we went. I said, "Thank you, Lord. That's the only good battery we have."

We arrived in Des Moines, Iowa, on the fourth day at about ten o'clock at night. We were all pretty tired and were anticipating getting into Indiana. I will never forget, as we were driving down a section of freeway that was down to one lane, the headlights on the bus went out. We were going about fifty miles per hour, and I couldn't see a thing! There was a semi-truck bearing down on us when it happened. We couldn't pull over because of the barricades on each side of us. When the truck driver saw what had happened, he turned on his bright lights and followed us for about five miles to the next exit. We pulled into a parking lot at a nearby mall and slept in the bus until morning. The next day we got an early start, and we traveled approximately eighteen hours before we pulled into my folks' place.

We had been in Indiana for nearly a week, and I candidated for the pastor's position in a church in Indiana. It was a beautiful, white, church building with a belfry; right in the middle of a field of corn. Some dear saint of God had donated one hundred thousand dollars to the church ten years earlier. Everything was paid for, the building, the parsonage, everything. These folks were looking for a pastor, and I was looking for a church, so we got together.

I'm afraid that all that money turned this particular church into a bunch of stiff-shirts. The only person who smiled at us was a little retarded lady, who lived across from the field of corn. You may know of a church like this, where no one smiles, or no one fellowship's. When we arrived, I was told when Sunday school started and when church started, then they sat down and stared at us. During the morning message I preached my heart out, and I told a couple of my best jokes, but no one cracked a smile or responded in any way.

After church service I had a meeting with the deacons (d-cons). They had a two and one half page of questions to ask me. They turned on a tape recorder to record every word I uttered. Some of the questions they asked were ridiculous. I didn't know the answers, and there was some question in my mind about whether or not God knew the answers. I realized, about midway through this interrogation, that these folks didn't want a pastor.

A NEW BEGINNING

During this time of waiting on the Lord I worked in a foundry. I just knew that the Lord was going to give me a place to serve Him. I was restless, not wanting to get too settled in anywhere, then I found another job in a rubber factory. My boss learned that I was a preacher. He was a playboy atheist, and I was putting a cramp in his style, so six weeks after I hired in, he fired me. I found another job in a fiberglass outfit twenty miles away.

By this time we were starting to become a little concerned about a place of service. My wife and relatives were concerned that I couldn't hold down a job. The fact of the matter was, I didn't want a job. I had gone to Bible College for four years, not to work in some factory, but to pastor a church. Eleven months later I found yet another job as a welder in a radiator shop.

By this time I had made contact with a preacher in Oregon. We had talked several times on the telephone and it was all set up. We were going to assume the responsibility of his church when he left. On the day we were to drive out there I called him on the phone. The pastor told me that there had been a tragedy at this church that very Sunday; someone had gotten run over in the church parking lot and was killed. We set another date for our meeting.

One day, while I was at work, one of the men, Don Heichel, came over to my work area at lunchtime. Don attended the same church I had when I got saved. He lived just down the street from our Cape Cod home fourteen years earlier. He gave me a newspaper clipping from a Christian newspaper, advertising a church in the state of Michigan that needed a pastor. I folded the clipping and stuck it in my pocket. I wasn't interested because we were going to Oregon in a couple of weeks.

I went home from work that Friday and told Margie, "We don't have anything else to do on Saturday, let's drive up to Michigan and look this church over." She said, "I thought we were planning to go to Oregon."

"It wouldn't hurt to look," I told her. So the next day we drove up to a little town called Langley, Michigan, where the population is nine hundred and two. We met the fellow who ran the ad in the newspaper, Tom Richardson, who owns a wholesale shop near Detroit. His wife, Barb, took us out to look the church building over. It is a beautiful little building with a beamed ceiling auditorium on a corner lot. It kind of reminds me of something one would see on "Little House on the Prairie." It has a full basement, new baptistry, piano, organ, and even pews! It is the only Baptist church in town.

We told the lady we thought it would be a nice place to start a church, but we were going to Oregon in a couple of weeks. On the way back to Indiana Margie said, "Maybe we ought to call Oregon and make sure everything is still going as planned." I told her that I had just talked to the preacher a couple of weeks earlier and everything was the same. But she said that she had one of her feelings, and insisted that I call. So to keep peace, I gave this fellow a call when we got home. His wife answered the phone. I told her that we were looking forward to meeting them when we moved out to pastor their church.

She said, "There must be a mistake, we hired a new pastor last week."

I asked her, "When were you folks going to tell us, after we drove eighteen hundred miles just to meet the new pastor?" I tried to be kind over the phone; too bad I wasn't talking to her husband.

There we were, with no hope of serving the Lord in Oregon. It looked as though the only door that was still open was the church in Langley. Seeing as how I had just gotten laid off from my welding job, we decided to take a closer look at the church in Michigan. On Monday, a friend of mine and I drove up to Langley and met with Tom Richardson. He and his wife have dedicated their lives and their business to help establish fundamental, soul-winning churches. They make a down payment on a building, repair or paint it, or whatever needs to be done, then wait for God to send a pastor. I had never heard of such a thing, and after the experience I had in the past I was quite skeptical, to say the least.

As I was conversing with Tom Richardson about the position of pastor, I kept waiting for the typical theological questions, or perhaps a meeting with the board of directors, or maybe a questionnaire. My friend, and Mr. Richardson, began talking about their businesses. Finally, after about an hour, I interrupted and said, "I don't mean to be rude, but let's get back to the business at hand, the church." It was getting late, and if there was going to be a series of questions to answer, I wanted to get it over with.

Mr. Richardson looked me in the eye and said, "There have been almost seventy inquiries about the position thus far. I've gotten calls from all across America. You want the church?" "Yes," I replied. He then reached into his pocket and gave me the keys to the building.

I couldn't believe what was happening. Then Mr. Richardson said, "I told my wife Saturday when you came up that you were going to be the pastor." About that time his wife came in, and he said, "Tell this guy who I said was going to be the pastor two days ago." She pointed at me. He then said, "After you've been in this business for awhile you just know." As we were leaving the parking lot of his business, he came over to the car and said, "Oh, by the way, Pastor, what name do we put on the church sign?" He didn't know my name, but he knew I was the one for pastoring this new church.

I went home and started packing. I went to my folks' house and got that old blue and white bus with Mickey Mouse painted on the side that we had driven across America. It felt good loading that old bus after thirteen months (and six jobs) waiting on the Lord. By this time we were financially drained. Now that we had a place to serve we couldn't afford to leave.

I prayed and asked the Lord to put in my mind the name of a person who could afford to lend us enough money to get us to Michigan. Sometimes when I get myself into these spots my pride tells me, "Don't be borrowing money, you will embarrass yourself." The name of Jim, my old motorcycle buddy from days gone by, seemed to keep popping up. Again my pride kept telling me, "What if he says no? You will look like a fool." If we could lead just one more person to the Lord on this new mission field, I'd take my chance of looking like a fool for Jesus. Dr. Ken Blue, in Seattle, once said, "There is no room in the ministry for pride." I gave Jim a call, and ten minutes later I not only had the money we needed, but the assurance that if we will do our best, God will do the rest.

We loaded that old bus up with everything we had. I have to admit it wasn't much, considering our twenty-three years of being married, and four children. By this time the muffler on the bus had rusted off, and it sounded like a freight train. Because of finances, the Lord opened a door allowing us to stay in a two- bedroom cabin at a local Bible camp, rent free, until we found a place to live.

On our second day in Michigan, Margie had a medical problem and had to see a doctor. The next day she had an allergic reaction to the medicine he had given her, so five miles and three hundred dollar ambulance bill later, she was given an injection to counteract the medicine she had taken. I knew we were in the Lord's will for sure, the Devil was up to his old tricks.

We were in the cabin for five months. It wasn't too bad except we didn't have any water at first and no heat. Most of our clothes were on the bus, so every time we needed something we would have to unload half the bus to get to it. During October, November and December we would turn the oven on in the kitchen and would heat the cabin that way. They had the first snow storm in that area on October 10 that year. We would have to shower in the main lodge a quarter of a mile away. It wasn't too bad going to the shower, but it was a possibility we could freeze to death on the way back. We had been in worse predicaments. Besides, souls were being saved at the church.

Finally, on December fifteenth of our first year, we were able to purchase a house in town for only five hundred dollars down. The house was fully furnished; the owner left everything behind, the sheets on the beds, the dishes in the cupboards, and the salt, and pepper shakers on the kitchen table. All we had to do was show up and move in. It was as if the Lord was saying, "Okay, Preacher, I know once again that you are relying on me. Welcome to Langley, Michigan.

BACK TO SQUARE ONE

The first thing I did upon our arrival in Langley was, like always, get a job to provide for the needs of my family. The Bible is still true: A man is worse than an infidel if he won't provide for his household.

I found a job working in a little machine shop, located in an old wooden barn. From the outside it didn't look like much, but inside there was thousands of dollars worth of machinery. The boss and I would go into some of the factories in the area and work on their equipment.

I was told when I hired in that paydays may be late from time to time, because of the paperwork being slow coming from the factories that was paying my boss. At first the paydays were almost always on time. Then around Christmas-time the boss told me he was having trouble with the payroll department in one of the factories, so that week 1 only received a fifty- dollar check. I was pre- warned that this would happen so I told Margie not to panic. The following week I received a check for one hundred dollars. We had to tighten our belts and make do.

One Sunday after church, I think it was an afternoon service, my boss' son asked to talk with me. He and his family had been attending our church for about two months.

He told me he knew someone who was a child molester and asked me what I thought he should do about it. I asked him a few questions to make sure he knew what he was talking about. I noticed that his wife had Margie in a corner talking to her.

I told him that he needed to contact the police or child protective service and that the parents needed to be notified immediately. I told him he needed to act soon for the sake of the children involved. The Bible is clear about those who would harm one of these little ones, that a millstone be hanged about their neck and that they be cast into the depths of the sea.

After they left from church, Margie and I was talking, and after we put two and two together we came up with four. The person they were talking about was my boss, his dad. I called him on the telephone to make sure we were right, and sure enough, it was true. Once again I reminded him what he had to do for the sake of the children.

The next morning I went to work, the boss seemed nervous. We had a few projects I was working on, so the boss left me alone in the shop. I told myself I couldn't work for this guy anymore. No doubt the word would get out, and in a town of nine hundred and two, it would get out, I couldn't take the chance of being identified with a child molester.

By this time, because of the short paydays the last couple of months, the boss owed me fifteen hundred dollars. He kept telling me the check was in the mail, but that didn't pay the bills. I made up my mind, fifteen hundred dollars or not, I couldn't work there any longer. I gathered all my tools and left a note telling the boss to send me my money as soon as it came in.

It is sad, but true, that in this day and age when the perverts of this world are demanding their rights. Many have entered into the last door of opportunity for these wicked people, the church. Unfortunately the average pastor today will allow anyone who appears willing to take a bus route, junior church, or a Sunday school class, to do so with no questions asked. Dear fellow pastor, take heed for the sake of your ministries, have them fill out an application showing past experience. Make sure that these people believe as you do, and make sure they are members of good standing for at least six months. Another precaution would be to have at least two adults in a classroom setting. Put windows on the nursery and classroom doors. All your church needs is one child abuse case against it and it could ruin your life's work.

The police were notified about the accusations, but I'm afraid his son and daughter-in-law must have changed their story. As far as I know he was under surveillance by the authorities, but nothing became of it.

There is one more authority that my old boss will have to face and His name is called Jesus. The O.J. Simpsons of this world may get by with murder, but there will be a payday someday!

YET ANOTHER JOB

I started looking for work immediately; it seemed like I've had a lot of jobs since that day in 1975. I found another job running a lathe on the midnight shift some twenty miles away. As usual, every new job was another mission field where I witnessed and tried to have a good testimony for the Lord.

One day, after about a year on the job, we were all in the washroom washing up. There had been a new man who had hired in about two months earlier. This guy had an awful foul mouth, he would curse about every other word. It has been said that the only way to judge a man is by what comes out of his mouth; that may be true.

We were washing our hands and this fellow was cursing every breath. Then to my surprise one of the fellows who was a weight lifter, and had muscles on top of muscles said, "We don't talk like that in front of the preacher man.

Boy was I ever surprised! I didn't even think that this guy liked me; and maybe he didn't, but he respected the stand I have taken for the Lord. Many people may not listen to you but they will watch the way you live. I have heard it said that your talk talks, and your walk talks, but you walk talks louder than your talk talks. How true it is. Never tell your children not to take up smoking while you blow smoke in their face. Dad used to tell me, "Don't do as I do, do as I say."

Then to my amazement this new fellow said, "I know all about that religious stuff. All you have to do is believe on Jesus and get saved." He told the men that he goes to church all the time. One minute he was talking like a sailor, and in the next breath he was preaching. I have to admit he threw me into a tailspin for a minute.

On the way home I had a long talk with the Lord about this new guy at work. The Lord seemed to impress upon me that, one can have a head knowledge of the things of God without a heart knowledge. Romans, chapter ten, verse nine states, *"That if thou shalt confess with thy mouth the Lord Jesus, and shalt believe in thine heart that God hath raised him from the dead, thou shalt be saved."*

This fellow had it in his head, but he missed it thirteen inches away in his heart. Also the Bible is clear that if you're a true child of God, old things are passed away and all things become new. If one doesn't repent, change his mind about his sin, and about God, *"ye shall all likewise perish."* Luke *13:3.*

Over the years I have had people tell me they were saved and baptized, and are members of a church, but the same people live like the Devil himself. They talk like the world talks, they dress like the world dresses, they smoke the same cigarettes as the world smokes, drink the same booze as the world drinks, and they attend the same ungodly movies as the world, so they must be of the world. The Bible states over and over to *"Wherefore come out from among them, and be ye separate, saith the Lord, and touch not the unclean thing; and I will receive you."* II Corinthians 6:17.

Hebrews 12:6 states, *For whom the Lord loveth he chasteneth, and scourgeth every son whom he receiveth. "* If a person is a Son of God, *John 1:12,* then the Lord will spank us when we are disobedient to His law. Just like the children of Israel throughout the Old Testament. When my children were growing up I spanked them because I loved them. I didn't spank the deacon's children, even though I would have liked to at times, why? Because they weren't mine. God only spanks His own.

NEW FACES NEW CHALLENGES

The church was coming along slowly, but we expected that, so we just kept being faithful. We went door-to-door soul winning, and telling people about the church, and of course, about the Lord!

One day we met a young man about twenty-five years old by the name of Jim Beam. Jim invited us inside, and after about an hour we led him to the Saviour. Jim had three children; two boys and one girl. His wife had divorced him a year before, and became a prostitute in Detroit.

Jim was a broken man. He was unemployed and on the verge of suicide. This poor guy was at his lowest. The only time he would attend church was when we went by and picked him up. He was a real introvert; the only time he spoke was when he was spoken to.

By this time we had a few more people attending church, most of them were unemployed and on welfare of one form or another. Don't get me wrong, these people are very precious to the Lord Jesus. But the hard facts are, if you don't pay the bills there won't be a church very long.

Every year the Richardson's would go to Hawaii for two or three months. Most of the time that would mean I was the only tither in this newly formed church.

We had a few folks, this one guy sticks out in my mind. He said he wanted to work for the Lord in our church. He was going to plant hedges around the church building, paint, and do whatever he could. I get excited when I hear that kind of talk.

Unfortunately, after a few months had passed it was apparent he was all talk and no walk. He quit coming to church on Sunday nights, and then started missing Sunday mornings. It wasn't long before he quit altogether. The Bible states something about those actions. If a person vows a vow unto God, it is better for that person not to make a vow, than to vow and not keep it. In other words, do what you say you are going to do.

One day a family called me on the phone inquiring about the church, and the times of the services. I was expecting them the next Sunday, but no new people showed up.

About two weeks later the family came to church, a man, a woman, and two teenagers. Come to find out, the husband, LeRoy, was about twenty-five years older than his wife, the teenagers were well mannered, so I thought to myself, alright, a new family to minister to.

This family came to church on a regular basis for quite awhile. One thing bothered me though, they would sit near the front, and the husband would raise his hand during the sermon and ask me questions that didn't have anything to do with the message.

The Bible tells us to avoid geneologies, and foolish questions that may cause young Christians to have doubt. You know what I'm talking about, for instance, who did Cain marry? Some people ask these questions to be cute, as was in LeRoys case. Others try to make you appear stupid. The philosophy of the world says, if I can make someone look stupid, then I will appear intelligent. Nothing is farther from the truth.

About this time we had another couple join our church. They told me that they were in a church that didn't do anything, and appeared to be dead. They were faithful almost from day one. I'm going to be as kind as possible as I describe this couple. They were the scroungiest people I had ever met. He worked on a hog farm and would leave work and come straight to church. Bless their hearts, their clothes were always wrinkled. Forgive me, but their breath was breathtaking.

It seemed, every time we had a visitor, they were the first ones to greet them. It has been said that first impressions are lasting impressions. I'm afraid that is true. This guy wanted to be a soul winner, and go out with me on Saturdays door to door to represent our church and the Lord Jesus Christ. Finally I had a talk with them in Christian love, explaining the importance of having a clean appearance for Jesus. The Richardson's even bought him a new white shirt, tie and slacks. This guy really looked sharp for about a month, but unfortunately he never washed or changed his shirt or tie. So after awhile it was worse than at the beginning.

These people lacked discipline in personal hygiene, but I believe they had a genuine desire to serve the Lord. God has a place for everyone; not everyone can be the pastor, or song leader, or usher, but everyone can be faithful. Eventually this couple moved away into the big city. They joined a large church that had bus routes going into the inner city, that is where they found their niche for the Lord.

We had a piano and organ in the church, but no player. Our daughter, Marla, plays them both, but had married a fine Christian young man a year or two before, and had moved away. Our daughter, Melissa, who was taking piano lessons, was limited on what songs she could play. One day a lady called me and asked if we had a piano player. I told her our piano player moved away. She asked if she could play for us. Of course I said yes; music is a very important ministry in the church. The next Sunday the piano player and her husband attended our church. They sang specials together; they even gave money when the plate went by. I thought to myself, now we'll get this church off the ground.

Things were going pretty good now that we had music, about twenty people, and the offerings were about one hundred dollars per week. The Lord was blessing us, even though LeRoy kept raising his hand in church asking questions, and the Jones' still left a lot to be desired in personal hygiene.

One day, after the morning service, our new piano player made a few questionable comments about that morning's message. She and her husband had come out of a different persuasion that we were used to. The following week she and her husband sang a special; it was nothing short of rock & roll.

About a month later, during the morning service, there was a teenager sitting on the front row. During my preaching he put his coat over his head and zipped it up. He looked like the headless horseman of Icabod Crane. I stopped preaching. I wanted to laugh, because he was pretty funny looking. I told him to sit up and pay attention. This young man had been coming to our church for about a year. I told him if he could sit up at school all day, he could sit up in the Lord's house.

After the final amen, the piano player approached me and started yelling at me, for picking on that poor, misunderstood, teenager. She said I didn't have any love and that these kids needed a place to come to where they wouldn't get scolded. The whole time she was punching me in the chest with her finger for emphasis.

I knew right then, we had a problem that had to be taken care of imme diately. I went home and prayed to the Lord to give me wisdom about what took place. As much as I hated to, my son, Adam, and I went to their house for a visit. I told her it would probably be for the best if they found a church where they could be comfortable.

One of the main reasons they started attending our church was because their church didn't let out until an hour after we did. They referred to themselves as "church tramps," going from one church to another. Remember, they said it, not me. Unfortunately there are some people with talent who think they have to be entertainers, not servants. Going from church to church, and sharing their blessings enables them not to feel guilty about not tithing, or teaching a class, or soul winning. Would God give us folks who just want to serve Him!

ONE STEP FORWARD
TWO STEPS BACK

Things were going very slowly at church. We lost our piano player and her husband. There ought to be a law that states a person can't use the telephone for six months if they leave a church. Two weeks later the Jones' moved (wrinkles and all) to the big city. So for all practical purposes we were back to square one.

One day while out soul winning I came across a house which had a sign on the door. The sign read; "Do not knock, you can't have money or cigarettes!" I was really curious, so I knocked on the door. A good-looking man about mid twenties answered the door. I asked him about the sign, and he said the neighbor kids were always bugging them.

To my surprise, the next Sunday, he and his wife, along with their son, came to church. To my further surprise, this guy had a job; he made good money in computers. After a month or so they both got saved and I baptized them.

Don and Marie came to church every time the doors were open. They really got involved in the Lord's work.

The following week an executive from Amtrak, and his wife joined our church. I got excited, now we had some stable families in the church, plus people were being saved and baptized. It seemed that two or three families would leave, then two or three families would join. During this time I still worked the mid-night shift some twenty miles away.

One Sunday morning I was preaching away and good old LeRoy raised his hand. I tried to ignore him, but he kept waving his hand. I stopped and said, "What's on your mind, LeRoy?" He said, "Hey preacher, how do you have sex in Heaven, fly by and smile?" His teenage son and daughter were so embarrassed they literally slid down in their pew.

I did the only thing I could do, I bowed my head and dismissed in prayer. As far as the Holy Spirit was concerned, church was over. His wife, bless her heart, just sit there and giggled. It is true the Devil will use anybody to disrupt a service, even ignorant people!

We extended our soul winning effort to the towns on either side of Langley. I felt myself getting beat down again, just like in Bellingham, Washington. I thought, perhaps if I got a day job, I would get more rest. I acquired another job in a factory where they built street rod, hot rod cars. My heart wasn't in it, but the bills needed to be paid.

One day at work I met a fellow who had graduated from a well- known Bible college down South. The first chance I got I mentioned something about the Lord to this fellow. He told me he was sick and tired of hearing about how the Lord is coming back. He told me that he wanted to enjoy life and not have to worry about all the do's and don'ts in the Bible.

I couldn't believe this guy. The college he graduated from was a well-known fundamental school, yet he didn't want any part of God, or me. I have found over the years that salvation is an individual thing, not the college, not the church, not the "doctor somebody" preacher, but the individual. I have seen it over and over, Godly parents have sacrificed to send their children to a Christian school or college, and the ungrateful brats won't even darken the doors of a church. Some even get rebellious against their parents, how sad.

THE BOTTOM FELL OUT

It was close to this time when our eldest daughter, Lori, who had been attending college in Pontiac, Michigan, met and fell in love with a preacher. They came to Langley to allow me the honor of performing the marriage ceremony. I was so proud, Lori, who was twenty-five years of age at that time, told me just before I walked her down the aisle that she was still a virgin. She had saved herself for her hero, Patrick Bishop. They now serve the Lord in the state of Georgia.

From time-to-time, in the ministry, a pastor will run across one who feels it is their duty to point-out all your faults in your ministry, and life. We had this one fellow who would visit our church about every six months, looking for something wrong so he could point it out to me.

Often these people are looking for faults in others hoping to justify their sin in their own life. Just the other day one of these people informed me my song leader had the playboy channel on his television. Of course I doubted it, but to satisfy this critic I checked it out. Only to find that it wasn't true after all. This very person was later found out to be an adulterer, and all-around con man.

Then approximately three years on this mission field, the bottom fell out. Jim, whom we had led to the Lord, and whose wife became a prostitute, was progressing gradually. Jim had a wonderful gift of teaching. He even came out of his shell and wrote poetry, and read it before the church.

One Sunday, we were going to have a picnic in the afternoon, and Jim was in charge of buying the meats. We gave him some money for the food, so on Saturday I thought I would check on him. It has been said that people don't do what you expect, but what you inspect. I went to his house, but no one was at home. His neighbor came over and told me Jim had moved to Chicago with his wife. I asked him, "What wife?" He told me the wife who had divorced Jim a couple of years before, and that she had been living with Jim for a couple of weeks.

A month later I received a letter from Jim telling me he had gotten back with his wife. He said they had moved to Chicago, then to Green Bay, Wisconsin. He had gotten a job working nights, but after a week or two, his wife had found a new boyfriend and moved in with him. Some things never change. The Bible states that the dog will return to its vomit.

Every year the Richardson's would go to Hawaii for about three months. And so it was again. One day Don and Marie came to me and he had a real burden to do more for the Lord. Don even talked about going to Bible College, and going into the ministry. I didn't notice it then, but his wife didn't have much to say on the subject.

A month or so later, the County Fair came to the area. Marie would place their son in a day care center, and then go to the fair. After four days of doing this, she ran off with the hot dog man. He was a complete stranger! When the carnival pulled out of town, she pulled out with it. It was unbelievable! Don came to me in tears; he was crushed. Funny thing was, his parents blamed it all on me. They said I was filling his head with going into the ministry.

Naturally in a little church like ours it was devastating. Don hired a private detective to track Marie down, then Don brought her home. Needless to say, that was the end of church for them and Don's parents. I have come to the place in my ministry where nothing surprises me anymore.

It has been said the average person influences at least three thousand people in a lifetime. When sin hits a family it affects all the family. Only eternity will tell why some people went to Hell. Gundi once said, he would have been a Christian if it weren't for Christians.

By then we were back to about three families, and a few other folks. It seemed as though there was one disaster after another, only this time they were leaving faster than they were coming in. I was drained spiritually and emotionally.

The town where we lived was very small. It had only one flashing light at the four way stop. Our church was on the only side street in town, and it was a dead end street.

One day I received a six-page letter from LeRoy, the fellow who wanted to know how to have sex in Heaven? In his letter he accused me of not coming to a complete stop at the only stop sign, next to the church, which was on a dead end street. He went on to tell me what a bad example I was for the teens in our church. It must have taken him hours to construct such a letter. Needless to say, I was dumbfounded at all the accusations in this letter written by a fellow who could barely write his own name.

Two days later I received an eight-page letter from the family who was an executive at Amtrak. It was almost word-for-word as LeRoy's letter. I marveled at this, here we have a fellow with a third grade education siding-up with an executive of one of the largest railroads in the world, just long enough to crucify the preacher.

As I ponder that situation I recall that the Pharisees and the Sadducees,

who wouldn't agree on anything, joined together just long enough to cru
cify my Lord. Needless to say, neither of them came back to church. Month's
later Margie and I were invited to go to the couple from Amtrak's house.
With tears they apologized for the slanderous letter, but by that time the end
was inevitable.

After almost five years we were back down to four or five women and
children. The bills were overwhelming on the house, and the church build-
ing. Reality had set in; we had been starved out.

We were forced to lock the doors on the church. We joined a church in
Detroit, some thirty miles away. After about three months I went to the
pastor and asked him if his church could give us enough money to rent a U-
haul truck, and fill it up with gas, we would appreciate it.

It was a weight I had put on my family and me, a weight I didn't want to
struggle with. Even a professional weight lifter may pull a muscle or sprain
his back. The only thing he can do is, to leave the weights, and become
nursed back to full strength. For my family and I it was a time to let the
wounds heal. I didn't even want to deal with this weight. I had developed
an attitude and I just didn't care.

So, we limped back to Indiana after almost five years on the Langley
mission field. We moved in with our daughter, Marla. She had gotten
married and moved to Indiana four years earlier. We were just going to be
there until I acquired another job, and had a couple of paychecks under my
belt.

Unfortunately, that took about three months. I had gotten bitter with the
way things had turned out. My children were upset and disappointed, be-
cause I had taken them out of yet another school, and they would have to
adjust to a new school. Margie was broken the most, and humanly speak-
ing, who could blame her?

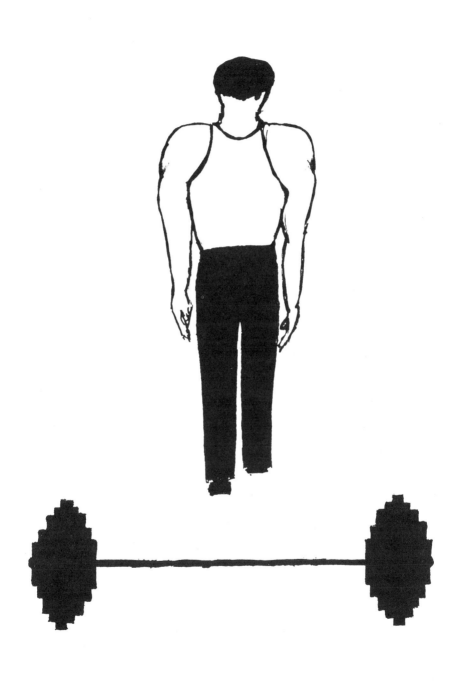

KNOCKED DOWN
BUT NOT KNOCKED OUT

Well, now we were back in Indiana where we had started out in that old blue and white bus, with Mickey Mouse painted on the side. I acquired yet another job working in a window factory, it didn't pay much, but it was close. I got to know some of the preachers in the area, and I preached every chance I could.

After about two months we received a call from a church in Salem Heights, Indiana asking me to fill the pulpit until they called a new pastor. By this time I had contacted a pastor in Green River, Wyoming. He was moving on and I was going to assume his pastorate. I wanted to get settled in somewhere before school started in the fall.

One morning we were getting ready to go to church and we discovered a letter from Melissa, our youngest daughter. She had run away during the night. She had been miss popularity at the little school in Langley, where the graduating class was forty-five students.

We had placed Melissa and Adam into this large school which had about two thousand students. I blame myself for this ordeal, after all, my children didn't stay in one school long enough to get to know any real friends. Missy was going to be a senior, and she wasn't happy about starting over.

Meanwhile, I was filling the pulpit in Salem Heights. Our first meeting we had only nine people, plus my family. The more I preached at Salem Heights, the more the door seemed to be closing in Green River, Wyoming. By this time I had gotten yet another job near the church in a carpenter's shop.

After a couple of weeks, we went back to Langley, Michigan, to look for Missy, who was then seventeen years old. I went to our old neighborhood, and asked our previous neighbor if he had seen her. He told me that she was marching in the school band, in the Labor Day Parade that went by his house the day before. He told us he had captured her on video- tape, so he played it for us, and sure enough there she was playing the drums. Unfortunately by the time we brought her back home our testimony for the Lord was destroyed in Langley, Michigan.

Adam and Missy attended the large school and hated every minute of it. Both their grades hit rock bottom, even though Adam rebounded his senior year. I prayed to the Lord to at least get them out of there with a diploma.

On Missy's eighteenth birthday, after graduation she packed all her belongings and moved in with her new friends. *Proverbs 13:20* states *"He that walketh with wise men shall be wise: but a companion of fools shall be destroyed."* I knew what was happening but, like most parents of teenagers, I didn't know how to stop it. I prayed for Missy every day. Some of you parents know what I am talking about, keep praying for your lost daughters, or sons, or wife, or husband. Never, and I mean **never** quit or give up on them. If we don't pray for them, in God's name, who will? It was a difficult time for Margie and I.

Six months after we discarded the weight put on us in Langley, Michgan, we picked it back up to try again. By this time I had assumed the pastorate position in Salem Heights, and the attendance went from nine to four in about three months.

Four months later Missy came home and was about three months pregnant. When something like that happens to preachers a lot of things go through their mind. I thought about resigning; but after all, she was eighteen now, and had been out of our house for about six months. I reasoned with myself, I couldn't follow my kids around with a baseball bat. So, with a lot of prayer, and help from the Lord, I continued as pastor.

SALEM HEIGHTS

By this time I had gotten another job in Michigan City, Indiana, making air filters. I worked days and the money was good. The church was giving me $185.00 per week. I didn't tell them, but that was $185.00 a week more than I received from our last church.

The church had a few things, such as, a piano, organ, chairs, copy machine, tables, and song- books. Their assets being about four thousand dollars. The building we met in was an old Methodist church, with a cemetery beside it. We tried to buy the building on a couple of occasions, but it was as if the Lord didn't want us to have it. Our offerings were around a hundred dollars per week, with the attendance in the twenties.

After about a year at Salem Heights, an elderly couple donated two and one quarter acres, a house, and an appliance store to the church. It would take tons of work and thousands of dollars before it could be used for the Lord's work. Unfortunately, some of the folks became concerned about who was going to do all that work, so we lost a few people during that time. We went into the ministry the same as all the other times; go soul winning, preach from the good old King James Bible, baptize folks, then teach them to go out and get some more.

A VAPOR IN TIME

I suppose after almost twenty-five years of one failure after another, even the most naïve person learns from his mistakes. I am convinced that the Lord's work is a spiritual work, it is the work of the Holy Spirit. True, we must prepare ourselves, but after we do our best, give the rest to God.

The only requirement for service, besides salvation, is faithfulness. We started working on the appliance store building in July. Our first work party about twenty-five people showed up to help clean up, tear up, and burn up. Someone suggested we video tape our progress as we went along, and so that is what we did.

One of the first major projects on the building was to replace the roof. By this time all the excitement had gone, and there were only a handful of people to work on the building. We had to remove the old roof before we could fix it.

One day Sylvia Thompson and I were on the roof pulling nails, Sylvia had been with the church from their first meeting. We were trying to get as much done before dark as possible, and it started to snow. I asked myself, what have I gotten myself into this time?

Finally, we hired a roofer to put a new roof on the building, unfortunately, he didn't know the first thing about flat roofs. When he finished, we had more leaks than when he began. More people became discouraged and left the church.

After four years our second daughter, Marla, her husband Doug Siebenhaar, along with three of our grandchildren, Titus, Bethany and Briann joined our church. Marla plays the piano, and Doug leads singing from time to time.

Our eldest daughter, Lori, and her husband, Patrick Bishop, are serving the Lord faithfully in a church in the state of Georgia. They are praying that God will give them a baby to raise for His glory. Patrick graduated from a

Bible college down there, and we are very proud of him and Lori both.

As I look back on life I realize that my grandchildren are about the same age of our children when we gave it all to Jesus back in 1975.

About this time a young man who had known Melissa, our youngest daughter, when she was about fourteen years old, seen her at his cousin's wedding. He had moved to Ohio for a few years, and then had been attending Bible College for a couple of years. They fell in love all over again. Our son-in-law, Patrick, and I performed their wedding ceremony. At the beginning of the wedding Patrick told of a dream that Don had had before he seen Missy at his cousin's wedding. He dreamt that he would meet a young woman, who had bore a child out of wedlock, and that he would marry her and raise the child as his own. Well, the child's name is Victoria Lynn, and Don and Melissa now have a child together by the name of Vanessa Mae. Don Tyson is not only our newest son-in-law, but he is a fine preacher.

The building program has progressed over the last three years. We went into the building program with a debt-free plan. In other words, if we couldn't afford something we didn't buy it. We haven't borrowed a dime on the project. Once a church in Tennessee heard about our building program, and sent us four hundred dollars. We acquired the ceiling tile in the main auditorium for free. All but one set of doors was donated to us. We have beautiful, leaded- glass entrance doors, with two side- lights, valued at approximately fifteen hundred dollars: The Lord led us to a garage sale where we bought them for twenty-six dollars.

The church has two central air units, which we purchased at almost half price. We have wall-to-wall carpeting that a fellow put down for almost nothing. I feel sorry for those folks who left our church before the blessings started to flow. Some have returned to enjoy the finished product, but they cannot appreciate it as much as the rest of us.

I suppose the church's total assets are now over $160,000.00, with plans

GETTING STRONGER

STRONGER   STRONGER

double the size of our present building.

We have seen hundreds of souls saved, and several dozen baptized in these five years. We support two missionaries, and are looking for more to support. I am still convinced church work is the Lord's work. It is a spiritual work. When people ask me how to start a church I can honestly say, "I don't know."

Since February 1, 1999 I have become the full-time pastor due to the glory of God. I have quit my job in the factory, and am now doing what God would have me to do. I didn't do anything different from the last two churches, but I believe the Lord is blessing our faithfulness over these last twenty-four years of service to Him. As I look at my life, I see the Lord Jesus has worked a miracle in my life and marriage. He has given me purpose, and direction, and He will do the same for you.

Our children are all grown now, and they all attend church regularly. I have had the privilege of performing the wedding ceremony of all three of our daughters to good, Godly, young men: two of which are preachers, and one is the best church layman one could ask for. Our son, Adam, who has stuck by my side through the good times as well as the bad, is now twenty years of age, and is a faithful servant of the Lord. I praise God for my children, and sons-in-law.

Our grandchildren can quote more scripture at six and four years of age than most Christians who have been saved for years. Our daughters have made Grandma and Grandpa hero's in the eyes of their children. They want to be just like us when they grow up, praise the Lord!

As you read this book, I hope you were encouraged by the exciting life the Lord has allowed us to live, with more adventures ahead. If your life seems unfulfilled or meaningless, or you have doubts about why you are here on planet Earth, or where you are going, take time to think about what is really important.

A VAPOR IN TIME

There is more to life than just beating your brains out to pay the bills, having a few children, gathering a few things along the way, then dying.

This I do know; Jesus loves you, He died for you, and arose again on the third day just for you. Why won't you make Him your Saviour today: If He is your Saviour, then make Him your Lord.

Remember, the weights in life can be used to make you stronger or, if you discard them, they will make you weaker. Ponder this: Success in the work of the Lord demands a lifetime of service.

Share the Inspiration

Give **Guideposts**

www.guideposts.com

Mail this card to start or renew your own subscription —give a friend a gift—or do both... And we'll surprise you with something special!

Send No Money — We'll Bill You Later!

1 YEAR $13.97	**2 YEARS $21.97**
plus $.97 delivery (12 issues)	plus $1.97 delivery (24 issues)
($13.97 plus $2.97 delivery for Canadian)	($21.97 plus $5.97 delivery for Canadian)

Your Name _____ (Please print)

Address _____ Apt. _____

City _____

State _____ ZIP _____

☐ Include my own subscription for ☐ Regular ☐ Large Print* ☐ One year ☐ Two years   01-202066508   PREFERRED SUBSCRIBER

Send a gift in my name to the person(s) named below:

Gift to: (Please print)	Gift to: (Please print)
Address _____ Apt. _____	Address _____ Apt. _____
City _____	City _____
State _____ ZIP _____	State _____ ZIP _____
☐ Regular ☐ Large Print* ☐ One year ☐ Two years	☐ Regular ☐ Large Print* ☐ One year ☐ Two years

Intended for the visually impaired   *A gift card will be sent in your name to the person(s) named above.*

|.''||||'''.|.|'''.|'.|'.|.||.||.||'.'||.''..|.||||'''.|

BUSINESS REPLY MAIL

FIRST CLASS MAIL   PERMIT NO. 38   CARMEL NY

POSTAGE WILL BE PAID BY ADDRESSEE

Guideposts®
PO BOX 856
CARMEL NY 10512-9994

(Please detach at perforation and mail card below)

*Thank You
for
your
support!*

Preferred Subscriber Guarantee

1. We guarantee that you may cancel your subscription(s) at any time upon request and that you will receive a prompt refund on any unserved issues.

2. We guarantee to continue your gift subscription(s) at the then current rate for as long as you wish, without interruption, unless you instruct us to stop.

3. We guarantee if you extend your own subscription we will also provide continuous service at the then current rate for as long as you wish.

4. Send no money now. As a Preferred Subscriber, a gift card will be automatically sent in your name every year (on receipt of payment) to the person named on the reverse side.

EPILOGUE

While I was in high school I had set a new high jump record, and was only an inch and a half away from setting the state record. I was only an inch and one half away from earning a track scholarship, to the college of my choice. I didn't take advantage of the opportunity at hand, the end result being I didn't set a state record, nor did I earn a track scholarship to the college of my choice.

For years, after graduating from high school, I had a dream, and the dream went something like this: I was running down an old country road outside my hometown. I had my sweats on and ankle weights on each ankle to help develop my leg muscles. My high school sweetheart (who is now my wife) was riding her bicycle beside me and she would say, "Only an inch and a half higher for a track scholarship to the college of your choice. Run faster, Larry, faster! Run harder, Larry, harder! Run farther, Larry, farther!" In my dream I would run faster, in my dream I would run harder, in my dream I would run farther. Often I would be awakened from this dream by the sound of jet aircraft landing on the flight deck above my head, for I was on board the U.S.S. Ranger, an aircraft carrier off the coast of Vietnam.

Reality would set in; I realized that I would never have another opportunity to set a new Indiana State high jump record. I would never again have another opportunity to earn a track scholarship to the college of my choice. I had my chance and I let it slip out of my hands. This dream haunted me for years after my high school days. Serving the Lord is comparable to that dream. We all have an opportunity to serve Him now, to win others to Christ now, and to dedicate our lives to Him now. Some day, just like my dream, we will wish we hadn't allowed the opportunity to slip by.

If this book has given you the realization that your time is brief, that you have only one chance, one lifetime to serve the Lord, then it has done its job.

The Bible states in James 4:14, *"Whereas ye know not what shall be on the morrow. For what is your life? It is even a vapor, that appeareth for a little time, and then vanisheth away."*